Instant Hymns

Instant Hymns

New texts to well-loved tunes
A Common Worship resource

MICHAEL
FORSTER

kevin
mayhew

Important Copyright Information

We would like to remind users of this book that the reproduction of any song texts without the permission of the copyright holder is illegal.

All the texts in this book are covered by the Christian Copyright Licensing (CCL) scheme. However, if you are *not* a member of CCLI, you must apply direct to Kevin Mayhew Ltd for permission.

If you would like more information regarding CCL, they can be contacted at the following address:

Christian Copyright Licensing (Europe) Ltd
PO Box 1339, Eastbourne, East Sussex, BN21 1AD

Tel: 01323 417711
Fax: 01323 417722
E-mail: info@ccli.co.uk

First published in 2002 by
KEVIN MAYHEW LTD
Buxhall, Stowmarket, Suffolk IP14 3BW
E-mail: info@kevinmayhewltd.com

9 8 7 6 5 4 3 2 1 0

ISBN 1 84003 968 X
ISMN M 57024 123 1
Catalogue No. 1500539

Cover design by Angela Selfe
Typeset by Richard Weaver

Printed and bound in Great Britain

Foreword

Making connections: that, for me, is one of the most stimulating aspects of theology. I remember the excitement the first time I noticed, for example, the parallels between the Moses story and the murder of the innocents in Matthew 2: by showing us the infant hidden away from a baby-murdering king and called 'out of Egypt' to lead his people to liberation, Matthew points us to Moses as a kick-starter for our understanding of Jesus.

The Hebrew and Christian scriptures are bursting with little 'Aha!' moments when some apparently insignificant small detail opens a whole wealth of meaning when connected with something else. The lectionary, with its groups of readings offers wonderful opportunities for this. So that was one reason for me to accept the invitation to write a hymn for every week, drawing together the main readings for the principal service and trying to express the essential meaning in ways that congregations can relate to easily – and sing easily, too, since they're all set to well-known tunes.

Another reason was perhaps to be a kind of 'liberator' myself. I know from experience what a time-consuming task selecting hymns for Sunday services can be: trying to cater for the diverse pastoral needs of the congregation, seeking a balance and variety of styles, metres, etc., and while doing this bearing in mind the particular liturgical needs of this day or that part of the service.

Please don't hear me as saying that selecting hymns is a chore: it's a time-consuming and sometimes difficult task, but immensely worthwhile when the choice enables congregations more fully to enter into the worship; more truly to bring the highs and lows, the celebrations and the tragedies that are our lives consciously into the presence of God.

Worship, of course, is much more than hymnody, but in most of our traditional patterns hymnody is a vitally important part of it. From the solemn Penitential tones of an 'Agnus Dei' to the sheer exuberance of 'Shine, Jesus, shine' (complete with the actions), it opens up avenues of active communication for worshippers. Who can begin to estimate the power of 'Eternal Father, strong to save' being sung by an impromptu gathering of sailors' families while wind and waves batter the coast? Hymnody is, for many people, the way in to worship, and that's why the weekly routine of selecting hymns is both a joy and a burden.

What I hope to have provided here is a resource, enabling a worship leader very quickly to find one of the hymns, confident that it will be appropriate for that specific Sunday.

Having found the text, there is just one more thing to do: consider the tune. The metre is given at the top of each text, so it shouldn't be too difficult – especially in the case of metres like 84 84 88 84 which as far as I know can only mean 'Ar hyd y nos' ('All through the night'). Others, like LM, give a wide choice, and it's worthwhile mentally to sing the text through before deciding. Hopefully, however, churches will be blessed with good musicians to whom that task can be delegated.

I hope these texts might enable congregations to participate in the whole of worship, and possibly, sometimes, to find some of those 'Aha!' moments from scripture that have opened up faith for me.

MICHAEL FORSTER

Year A

The First Sunday of Advent

1 CM

1. Waken, O sleeper, wake and rise,
   salvation's day is near,
   and let the dawn of light and truth
   dispel the night of fear.

2. Let us prepare to face the day
   of judgement and of grace,
   to live as people of the light,
   and perfect truth embrace.

3. Watch then and pray, we cannot know
   the moment or the hour,
   when Christ, unheralded, will come
   with life-renewing power.

4. Then shall the nations gather round
   to learn his ways of peace,
   when spears are turned to pruning-hooks,
   and all our conflicts cease.

The Second Sunday of Advent

2 98 98

1. Behold, the Saviour of the nations
   shall spring from David's royal line,
   to rule with mercy all the peoples,
   and judge with righteousness divine!

2. He shall delight in truth and wisdom,
   with justice for the meek and poor,
   and reconcile his whole creation,
   where beasts of prey shall hunt no more.

3. Here may his word, with hope abounding,
   unite us all in peace and love,
   to live as one with all creation,
   redeemed by mercy from above.

4. Prepare the way with awe and wonder;
   salvation comes on judgement's wing,
   for God will purify his people,
   and 'Glory!' all the earth shall sing.

The Third Sunday of Advent

3 10 10 11 11

1. The Saviour will come, resplendent in joy;
   the lame and the sick new strength will
   enjoy.
   The desert, rejoicing, shall burst into flower,
   the deaf and the speechless will sing in
   that hour!

2. The Saviour will come, like rain on the earth,
   to harvest at last his crop of great worth.
   Await him in patience, with firmness of
   mind;
   both mercy and judgement, his people
   will find.

3. The Saviour will come, his truth we shall
   see:
   where life is renewed, and captives set fee.
   No finely-clad princeling, in palace of gold,
   but Christ with his people, O wonder
   untold!

The Fourth Sunday of Advent

4 87 87

1. The sign of hope, creation's joy
   is born of purest beauty:
   the virgin's womb, now glorified,
   where grace unites with duty.

2. Immanu-el shall be his name,
   a title pure and holy,
   for God with us will truly be
   among the poor and lowly.

3. Where love divine concurs with trust
   to share redemption's story,
   Emmanu-el is born in hope,
   and earth exults in glory.

4. Now we, by grace and duty called,
   proclaim to every nation
   the Sign of hope which Mary bore,
   and promisc of salvation.

Christmas Day: Set 1

5 87 87 87

1. Those who walked in deepest darkness
   see at last a splendid light
   heralding a Son now given,
   born of God to human sight.
   He will reign in peace for ever,
   setting every wrong to right.

2. Shepherds hear the angels calling,
   telling of a newborn King
   lying in a straw-filled manger;
   O, the awesome song they sing!
   'Glory in the highest heaven!'
   All the world with joy will ring!

3. Now, the work of grace completed,
   all creation reconciled,
   let us live in Godly freedom,
   not as slaves by sin defiled;
   seek again the greater glory
   once revealed in Mary's child.

Christmas Day: Set 2

6 10 10 10 10

1. Proclaim good news: God's people have
   been saved,
   this day salvation dawns upon the earth.
   Build up, build up the highway for the Lord,
   proclaim God's majesty, and human worth!

2. Proclaim good news: new life is flowing
   free,
   not by our goodness but by God's own
   grace,
   through Jesus Christ, our Saviour and our
   Lord:
   he pours his Spirit into every place.

3. Proclaim good news: great joy to all the
   world,
   to us is born a Saviour, Christ the Lord.
   'Glory to God!' the angel host proclaim.
   'And peace on earth!' we cry with one
   accord.

Christmas Day: Set 3

7 87 87 87

1. Lovely feet upon the mountains
   bring the distant runner near,
   with the word of true salvation,
   set to gladden every ear.
   Sing for joy, you ransomed people,
   God has made the vision clear.

2. Now in even greater glory
   comes the co-eternal Word,
   he through whom, in primal darkness,
   first creation's breath was stirred.
   All the glory of the Godhead
   in his form is seen and heard.

3. He, the Father's very image,
   came to save and justify,
   then, the full atonement finished,
   took his proper place on high.
   Now his name, with awe and wonder,
   all the angels glorify.

The First Sunday of Christmas

8 87 87 87

1. Holy Jesus, in our likeness,
   born a human home to share,
   you who knew a father's kindness
   and a loving mother's care,
   by your ever-present mercy,
   may we catch this vision fair!

2. Christ who came to be a brother
   to each mortal family,
   by your sharing in our struggles,
   fit us for eternity!
   Saviour, hold your many people
   in your Spirit's harmony.

3. Let us celebrate your presence
   in our lives at every stage,
   passing on your wondrous story,
   faithfully, from age to age;
   trusting every generation,
   with this holy heritage!

The Second Sunday of Christmas

9 84 84 88 84

1. Word made flesh, eternal Wisdom
born from above,
light and life of all creation,
perfect in love;
faithful to the Father's sending,
perfectly our nature blending
by the Spirit's power, attending
as holy Dove.

2. Come to call your faithful people
from ev'ry place,
come to make our hearts your temple,
radiant with grace;
come, the Father's love revealing,
to our wayward souls appealing,
'til, within his presence kneeling,
we see his face.

3. Blessèd be our God and Father,
Saviour and Lord,
calling us to be his children
still by his Word,
who before the world's foundation
planned our undeserved salvation;
hail him God of all creation,
ever adored!

The Epiphany

10 86 88 6

1. Arise to greet the Lord of light,
you people of his choice.
In uncreated glory bright,
he bursts upon our inward sight,
and bids the heart rejoice! *(2)*

2. Towards his light shall kings be drawn
this majesty to see,
and in the brightness of the dawn,
shall see the longing world reborn
in justice full and free. *(2)*

3. The holy light in Judah's skies
calls sages from afar.
Great minds in meek obedience rise,
and call the world to recognise
creation's guiding star! *(2)*

4. This majesty for long concealed
from longing human sight,
in Jesus Christ is now revealed,
and God's eternal promise sealed
in love's unending light. *(2)*

The Baptism of Christ

11 LM

1. Behold the Servant of the Lord,
the chosen one, his soul's delight,
within whose heart the Spirit dwells
who brings true righteousness to sight.

2. He will not raise his voice aloud,
nor do to death the struggling flame,
but bring forth justice on the earth,
and nations all shall own his name.

3. The great baptismal act is done,
now hear the thunder from above,
and see the co-eternal Son,
resplendent in the Father's love.

4. So now to all the world proclaim
the news of universal grace,
and let the name of Christ be known
in every nation, tribe and race.

The Second Sunday of Epiphany

12 67 67 66 66

1. Thus says the Lord of hosts
to his belov'd creation,
'My servant I commend,
a light for every nation.
My people he will call
from every time and place,
and wholeness, my desire,
this broken world embrace.'

continued

2. Behold, the Lamb of God,
our sinful souls befriending.
The Spirit is his sign,
in pow'r and grace descending.
Of higher nature he
than all who went before,
to heal and save the lost,
with perfect grace in store.

3. Now may the Father's grace,
to all the world be given,
through his eternal Son,
with perfect peace of heaven.
O fellowship divine,
and love's eternal spring,
your never-ending praise
let all creation sing!

The Third Sunday of Epiphany

13 87 87 47

1. Sing to God a song of gladness,
tell his glory, all the earth;
robed in truth and full of beauty,
he who wrought creation's birth!
Alleluia! Alleluia!
Laud and honour are his worth! *(2)*

2. Once in deepest darkness living,
we have seen a wondrous light;
all the brightness of salvation
bursts upon our waiting sight!
Alleluia! Alleluia!
See the darkness put to flight! *(2)*

3. From the pride and predilections
which the holy church divide,
we are called to true communion
in the light of him who died.
Alleluia! Alleluia
to the Saviour crucified! *(2)*

The Fourth Sunday of Epiphany

14 LM

1. Christ, whose abundant grace transformed
plain water into glorious wine,
transfigure our communion, now,
and let us feast on love divine.

2. Your deep, mysterious grace is shown
in those who seem to have the least,
yet gladly give their meagre all
for you to turn into a feast.

3. In perfect wisdom, you have called
the 'nothings' whom the proud despise,
and those we count of little worth
you use to shame the worldly-wise.

4. So may our only wisdom be
the folly of the Crucified;
let justice be our one desire
and Christ himself our only pride.

The Presentation of Christ in the Temple

15 87 87 D

1. Oh, the wonder of the ages,
God is held in mortal hands,
offered in an earthly temple
to fulfil the law's demands!
With what grace, immortal Being
shares our flesh and draws our breath,
by his life true life imparting,
by his death, destroying death.

2. Lord, transform our earthly temples
with your covenant of grace,
make us ready for your coming,
fit to stand before your face.
By your own refining presence,
come to purify and bless,
that our lives may be an off'ring
full of truth and righteousness.

3. Come, then, Lord, in grace and judgement,
shaming all our greed and pride,
to the broken and exploited,
all the world has cast aside.
Come, your very self to offer
to the greatest and the least,
then present us to the Father,
Christ, our brother, Saviour, Priest.

Sunday between 3 and 9 February inclusive
(if earlier than the Second Sunday before Lent)

Proper 1

16 **10 11 11 12**

1. Come, let us worship the Lord of our birth,
who stretched out the heavens and
founded the earth;
his love never falters, his mercy is sure;
in hope ever faithful shall his kingdom
endure.

2. Christ bids us serve him as salt and as light,
to make of creation a feast of delight,
for justice and mercy should flavour the
earth,
and salt bland and tasteless is devoid of all
worth.

3. Wholeness and health in creation restore,
give bread to the hungry and shelter the
poor;
find clothes for the naked, relieve the
oppressed,
and thereby discover, one who blesses is
blessed!

4. O may the gospel so simply be told,
no artful philosophy here to unfold!
We nothing need know but the death of
the Lord,
and trust not in words, but in the pow'r of
the Word!

Sunday between 10 and 16 February inclusive
(if earlier than the Second Sunday before Lent)

Proper 2

17 **98 98**

1. O holy wisdom, gracious offer
of curse or blessing, life or death!
We choose the joy of holy living,
enlivened by the Spirit's breath.

2. This wisdom, ev'ry law surpassing,
comes not to cancel or replace,
but breaks the bounds of legal contracts
and frees our minds to live by grace.

3. We live as people of the Spirit,
in whom our peace and friendship grow,
and give to God alone the glory,
whose free abundant grace we know.

4. Praise Father, Son and Holy Spirit,
eternal, blessed One-in-Three;
our strength, our guide, our pure salvation,
the wisdom of the Trinity.

Sunday between 17 and 23 February inclusive
(if earlier than the Second Sunday before Lent)

Proper 3

18 **87 87 87**

1. Holy God, eternal Father,
we, your church, would holy be.
As your temple, here we gather;
keep us from all malice free.
Alleluia! Alleluia!
Grant us here your face to see.

2. In your saving pow'r rejoicing,
we would sing eternal praise,
all our hope and homage voicing,
holy God of endless days.
Alleluia! Alleluia!
Truth and mercy are your ways.

continued

3. Holy Wisdom, now transcending
all the strictures of the law,
from the legal code unbending
set us free to love you more!
Alleluia! Alleluia!
Perfect fellowship restore.

4. Holy God, eternal Father,
we, your church, would holy be.
As your temple, here we gather,
now by grace and faith set free.
Alleluia! Alleluia!
Let us live abundantly!

The Second Sunday before Lent

19 DSM

1. 'Let there be glorious light!'
rings out the word of grace,
and dark, unfathomed deeps become
creative light and space.
Then, 'Let the depths give forth!'
the word, with living pow'r,
invites creation to become
and gen'rously to flow'r.

2. Breath of the living God,
by whom the Word is known,
through whom creation comes to birth,
and love's great hope is shown,
O breathe within our hearts,
to set our spirits free,
and from those awesome depths bring forth
the people we might be.

3. 'Let there be glorious light!'
O breathe the Word of grace,
and bring to our chaotic lives
creative light and space.
Then help us trust the love
that lets us truly be,
and glories in the sight and sound
of spirits fully free.

The Sunday next before Lent

20 DCM

1. The glory of the living God,
on Sinai's mount, was shown,
though not contained in written word
on bare, unyielding stone;
for forty days and forty nights,
the fire of hope foretold
that greater Word, that nobler grace
than law can ever hold!

2. Another time and mountaintop;
the glory stands revealed:
the long-awaited Word of grace
in flesh and blood concealed!
Here Moses and Elijah stand,
the prophet and the law,
with him who, by the Spirit's fire,
their glory will restore!

3. The written word on lifeless stone,
the light within the cloud,
await a greater glory yet,
with grace and truth endowed.
The Word made flesh in Christ reveals
the majesty divine,
whose face, with uncreated light,
eternally will shine!

Ash Wednesday

21 87 87 D

1. Holy God, of righteous glory,
see your people gathered here,
in a solemn congregation,
your forgiving word to hear.
God of love and slow to anger,
gracious, longing to restore,
hear your priests and people calling,
give us grace to sin no more.

2. We confess the pride we suffer,
needs which none can satisfy;
how we love the praise of mortals,
swift to flow'r and quick to die.
Let us find rewards eternal
as we quietly seek your face,
and our open, public living
witness only to your grace.

3. Free us from our self-bound living,
better witnesses to be,
to the world by grace appealing
telling forth the mystery:
how creation's pure Redeemer
walked among us undefiled,
by his deathless love proclaiming,
God with us is reconciled.

The First Sunday of Lent

22 10 11 11 12

1. Lord of creation, forgive us we pray
for choosing to tread Adam's mutinous way;
subdue our ambitions and restless desires,
and open our hearing to the Word who inspires.

2. Sad and bereft, oh what beauty we lose
in treating creation as ours to abuse!
O how we exploit her for profit and gain,
not hearing her protest, nor aware of her pain!

3. Keep our religion from poison and stain,
and let us not use it for glory or gain;
refocus our vision, our worship restore,
as you and you only we exalt and adore.

4. Point us to Christ, in whose passion we see
forgiveness and mercy both priceless and free.
At last may we stand in the light of his face
in kinship created, and forgiven by grace.

The Second Sunday of Lent

23 98 98

1. In every time, in every nation,
God's call to Abraham is heard,
and faithful people rise and follow
by faith in God's unfailing word.

2. In Christ, that Word, was made incarnate,
who came in perfect grace and love
to bring, by water and the Spirit,
the gift of new life from above.

3. All praise to God, whose gracious mercy
can count our faith as righteousness,
and spread the promise of salvation
to all the world he longs to bless.

The Third Sunday of Lent

24 10 10 11 11

1. O God of all truth, forgive us we pray,
for doubting your love, and fearing your way.
Renew by your mercy the spirit within,
and flood with submission the dryness of sin.

2. This gospel of grace is ours to proclaim:
Christ Jesus restores from sin and from shame,
you give us the water of freedom to share,
the broken find healing and love past compare.

3. O mercy profound, ineffable grace!
The fullness of love is seen in his face.
He died for us sinners while sinful we stood
who, saved by his passion, are counted as good.

The Fourth Sunday of Lent

25 77 77 77

1. Holy Shepherd, King divine,
   meet us in this holy place;
   gather all our wayward hearts
   in the warmth of your embrace.
   Here accept the praise we sing,
   and the humble gifts we bring.

2. God who chose and crowned as King
   one who played the shepherd's part,
   unimpressive to the eye,
   but of true and faithful heart:
   look on every upturned face
   with your own all-seeing grace.

3. Holy Shepherd, set us free
   from the terrors of the night;
   open now our sightless eyes,
   let us see creation's Light,
   and with all the world rejoice
   as the Spirit gives us voice!

Mothering Sunday

26 SM

1. O God of perfect love,
   your promises we own,
   that through a mother's tender care
   your glory can be shown.

2. Then give us faith to know
   your word will never fail:
   the troubles of the present day
   a brighter future veil.

3. The temple prophet speaks,
   and we his vision see,
   of pain and blessings both to come
   in every family.

4. May Mary's faith be found
   in ev'ry human heart,
   to wonder at the mystery
   and play our humble part.

The Fifth Sunday of Lent

27 11 11 11 11

1. O God of our fathers, almighty to save,
   come rescue our spirits from sin's early grave.
   Enliven our souls with the promise of grace
   and give us the courage new life to embrace.

2. Though deeply entombed in the cavern of shame,
   we thrill to the Saviour who calls us by name;
   released from despair and assured of our worth,
   we welcome with rapture the call to come forth!

3. Now, freed from enslavement to sin and to death,
   we sing of this grace as the Spirit gives breath,
   and order our lives, both in action and word
   as those who are sharing the joy of the Lord.

4. All honour and glory to Father and Son,
   and life-giving Spirit, eternally one,
   whose promise of perfect salvation we know
   and from whose abundance true freedom will flow.

Palm Sunday: Liturgy of the Passion

28 SM

1. What dreadful sight is this,
   by fear and envy wrought,
   the faithful servant of the Lord
   in pain and death distraught!

2. But God will give him strength,
   with patience to endure,
   and bring him through this time of trial
   in word and action pure.

3. And now, before our eyes,
 a myst'ry so divine;
 redemption's wondrous story, told
 in broken bread and wine!

4. The co-eternal Son,
 in splendour bright arrayed,
 for us his glory set aside
 and unto death obeyed.

5. Exalted over all,
 and giv'n the highest name,
 him shall all nations, kings and powers
 eternally acclaim.

Maundy Thursday

29 14 14 4 7 8

1. God of the Passover, Author and Lord of salvation,
 gladly we gather to bring you our hearts' adoration;
 ransomed and free,
 called and commissioned to be
 signs of your love for creation.

2. Here we remember that evening of wonder enthralling,
 myst'ry of passion divine, and betrayal appalling.
 Breaking the bread,
 'This is my body,' he said.
 'Do this, my passion recalling.'

3. God of the Eucharist, humbly we gather before you,
 and, at your table, for pardon and grace we implore you.
 Under the cross,
 counting as profit our loss,
 deep in its shade, we adore you.

Good Friday

30 84 84 88 84

1. Day of wrath and day of wonder,
 whence hope has fled!
 See the body torn asunder,
 blood freely shed.
 Stripped of majesty we saw him,
 human sight recoiled before him,
 yet it was our sorrows tore him;
 for us he bled.

2. Day of hope and day of glory,
 though unperceived!
 See redemption's dreadful story,
 long, long conceived.
 Evil pow'rs, in tatters lying,
 knowing death itself is dying,
 hear the voice triumphant crying,
 'All is achieved!'

3. Day of majesty and splendour,
 here ends the race!
 Christ, our Priest, our souls' defender,
 longs to embrace.
 He who walked this earth before us,
 tried and tempted, yet victorious,
 calls us to the kingdom glorious.
 O, perfect grace!

Easter Day

31 CM or 86 86 extended

1. To him who died is now restored
 the life he freely gave.
 We worship here the Lord of life,
 now risen, risen, risen,
 risen from the grave!

2. The misty light of early dawn
 reveals an empty cave.
 How vain to search the tomb for one
 now risen, risen, risen,
 risen from the grave!

continued

3. His were the hands that healed the sick,
   and made the fearful brave.
   Though once despised, his power we see
   now risen, risen, risen,
   risen from the grave!

4. The pleasures of this passing age
   cannot our souls enslave;
   for true contentment rests with him,
   now risen, risen, risen,
   risen from the grave!

5. To all creation, we proclaim,
   'The pow'r to heal and save
   is vested in the living Lord
   now risen, risen, risen,
   risen from the grave!'

The Second Sunday of Easter

32 76 76 D

1. Blest be the God and Father
   of Jesus Christ our Lord,
   for hope to sinners given
   through his unfailing word;
   the promise of redemption
   eternally is sealed,
   and Christ in deathless glory
   by broken tomb revealed.

2. In many signs and wonders,
   his Godly state was shown,
   yet such a Son of David
   the world chose not to own.
   When worldly pow'rs condemned him
   to torture, cross and grave,
   God raised him up and crowned him
   with cosmic pow'r to save.

3. Although we have not seen it,
   his promise we believe;
   what minds can never capture
   our hearts by faith receive.
   Our spirits thirst with longing,
   like infants at the breast,
   to see the Saviour's glory,
   and in his presence rest.

The Third Sunday of Easter

33 LM

1. The risen Lord we now confess
   as him the world has once denied,
   since God has made both Christ and Lord
   the one his people crucified.

2. And yet his deathless promise stands
   for all who turn from godless ways,
   his own life-giving Spirit waits
   to fill our lives with hope and praise.

3. Though scorned, betrayed and done to
   death,
   the grave could not his life confine;
   he scorned its pow'r and burst its seal,
   and meets us here in bread and wine.

4. The Lord has walked our lonely road,
   and shared the fear we all have known.
   He breaks with us the bread of life,
   whereby his presence still is shown.

5. Forsaking all our vain desires,
   the saving blood of Christ we claim.
   In rev'rent fear and holy joy,
   we call upon the Father's name.

The Fourth Sunday of Easter

34 87 87 87

1. Christ, in risen pow'r triumphant,
   let your life be fully known:
   in the church, your risen body
   let the love of God be shown,
   nothing sparing, all things sharing,
   counting nothing as our own.

2. Patiently for us he suffered;
   all the lost are his concern.
   Innocent, he bears our sorrow;
   his forbearance we may learn.
   Now confiding, nothing hiding,
   to the Shepherd we return.

3. Still the risen Saviour calls us;
   we must freely make our choice.
   Gladly will we rise and follow,
   knowing well the Shepherd's voice,
   calling, leading, for us pleading,
   where the saints in light rejoice.

The Fifth Sunday of Easter

35 DCM

1. The temple of the living God
   is built of living stones,
   a holy people, called to live
   by light of Christ alone.
   With special joy we celebrate
   the word the psalmist said,
   'The stone the builders cast aside
   is now the corner's head!'

2. The temple of the living God
   is set secure above,
   where Christ invites the world to share
   his perfect reign of love.
   And we who seek the Father's face
   are summoned to obey,
   and follow where he goes before,
   the Life, the Truth, the Way.

3. The temple of the living God,
   where Christ in glory stands,
   will challenge all our loyalties
   to temples built with hands.
   Then, let the Holy Spirit's pow'r,
   unlock our earthbound sight,
   to see beyond these darkened halls
   to Christ's eternal light.

The Sixth Sunday of Easter

36 CM

1. Let all the world exultant sing
   in holy harmony,
   and constant alleluias ring
   to God, who sets us free.

2. We own the name of Christ, who died
   in agony and shame,
   now by the Spirit glorified
   with heaven's highest name.

3. His is the name by which we live,
   his passion we embrace,
   and glory to the Saviour give
   for his abundant grace.

4. The God of myst'ry, long unknown,
   in Christ has been revealed.
   In him we live, and move, and are,
   in him our life is sealed.

5. Let all the world exultant sing,
   in holy harmony,
   by word and action honouring
   the blessed Trinity.

Ascension Day

37 87 87 87

1. Hail the risen Christ, ascending
   to his holy Father's side;
   angels, lost in awe and wonder,
   now acclaim the Lord who died.
   Alleluia!
   Christ triumphant, glorified.

2. He who once, from royal splendour,
   came to share our state of blame,
   now ascends in clouds of glory
   to the heights from which he came.
   Alleluia!
   Christ for evermore the same!

3. He will grant his praying servants,
   from the riches of his pow'r,
   grace to life as risen people,
   in this present watching hour.
   Alleluia!
   God on us his blessings show'r.

continued

4. Now, he bids us tell his story,
   where the lost and fearful roam:
   he will come again in glory,
   and will lead his people home.
   Alleluia!
   Maranatha! Come, Lord, come.

The Seventh Sunday of Easter

38 11 11 10 11

1. Father, bless your people, that we may be one,
   sharing in the glory of your only Son;
   held and forgiven, reconciled by grace,
   knowing life eternal, here in time and space.

2. In these special moments, lightly we may pray;
   but in humbler service, faithful let us stay,
   and, when we gather in the simplest place,
   show us in each other your incarnate face.

3. When we face injustice for the faith we claim,
   let us know we suffer in the Saviour's name.
   Victims forgotten, innocents accused,
   know the silent protest of their Christ abused.

4. Praise the blessed Father, and eternal Son,
   praise the Holy Spirit, ever Three-in-One.
   Perfect Communion, rich diversity,
   essence of creation, blessed Trinity.

Day of Pentecost

39 87 87 D

1. Holy Spirit, to us given
   at the Pentecostal feast,
   Breath of God and fire of heaven,
   promise of our great High Priest,
   fill our hearts with joy and wonder
   in this special Sabbath hour,
   burst the locks of fear asunder,
   send us out with risen power.

2. Holy Spirit, love undying,
   promise of the risen Lord,
   all your power unifying
   breathes in his eternal word.
   Pour on us your special blessing,
   members many, body one,
   Jesus Christ as Lord confessing,
   he the co-eternal Son.

3. Holy Spirit, in us living,
   vigour of the risen Lord,
   to our mortal bodies giving
   life, by sacrament and word,
   send us to the warring nations,
   to a world by sin defiled,
   with the gospel of salvation:
   all creation reconciled.

Trinity Sunday

40 86 88 6

1. Oh, who can know the mind that planned
   the making of the earth,
   who held the waters in his hand,
   and weighed the isles like grains of sand,
   and brought all life to birth! *(2)*

2. The Word he breathed in time and space
   now calls us to proclaim,
   for every nation, every race,
   the promise of his saving grace
   in ev'ry age the same. *(2)*

3. With joy and praise, eternally,
   creation will resound,
   to Father, Son and Spirit, three,
   one undivided Trinity,
   O Mystery profound! *(2)*

Sunday between 29 May and 4 June inclusive (if after Trinity Sunday)

Proper 4

41 SM

1. O look upon us, Lord,
   be merciful and kind,
   and may our sin and anarchy
   your true compassion find.
2. We long to keep the law,
   in which your love is known,
   to follow in the way of truth
   and trust in you alone.
3. And yet, this truth we know:
   the law cannot atone;
   the sinner will be justified
   by grace and faith alone.
4. So on this rock we stand,
   and to it make appeal:
   our faith in Jesus crucified,
   and him our sign and seal.
5. O give us grace to know
   the Saviour's faithful ways,
   to live in sacrificial love
   and offer worthy praise.

Sunday between 5 and 11 June inclusive (if after Trinity Sunday)

Proper 5

42 77 77 77

1. Come, O God, like morning light,
   bringing judgement clear and bright;
   come like water on the earth,
   calling life and hope to birth;
   come in judgement and in grace,
   where your people seek your face.
2. God, whose promise was received
   when the patriarch believed,
   now your waiting people bless,
   counting faith as righteousness,
   sinners only justified
   by the blood of one who died.
3. Let the love our lives express
   prove the faith our lips profess;
   may we hold, with special grace,
   those the world will not embrace.
   In the people most denied,
   let us serve the Crucified.

Sunday between 12 and 18 June inclusive (if after Trinity Sunday)

Proper 6

43 11 11 11 11

1. O God of the wilderness, mountain and plain,
   who rescued your people from slav'ry and pain,
   your goodness and grace in our hearts are made known,
   a kingdom and priesthood you choose as your own.

2. This gospel of joy to the world we proclaim:
   the grace of the Saviour is ever the same.
   The sick he will heal and the dead he will raise,
   and all of creation resound to his praise.

3. O wonder! O glory! O myst'ry unknown!
   What merciful goodness the Saviour has shown.
   He suffered for us, who by sin were defiled,
   and now counts us good, by his death reconciled.

4. O God of the exodus, God of the cross,
   you rescue your people at measureless cost!
   Through death and through desert you travel before;
   in faith let us follow, to praise and adore!

Sunday between 19 and 25 June inclusive
(if after Trinity Sunday)

Proper 7

44 666 66 and refrain

1. Sing to God, praise the Lord!
O what grace in his word!
Hope of peace he affords,
lifting up the lowly,
bringing judgement holy.

God is good, good, good,
God is good, good, good.
God our strength, God our song,
God our guide for ever.

2. Jesus came, full of grace,
light and truth in his face,
to redeem Adam's race,
conquered death in dying,
perfect grace supplying.

3. He will come, have no fear,
all that's hid will be clear,
trust his love ever near,
grace and truth abounding.
Hear his praise resounding:

Sunday between 26 June and 2 July inclusive

Proper 8

45 LM

1. O come all nations, celebrate
the solemn promise of the Lord,
of peace established in the land
and exiled refugees restored.

2. In Christ we have the promise sealed,
who gives us deeper peace within,
and rescues with his saving grace
his people once enslaved to sin.

3. We meet him in the stranger's face,
when simple care and love are shown,
and in the giving of his peace,
the perfect grace of Christ is known.

4. Then let the nations shout with joy
and, with a voice of singing, praise
the one from whom all goodness flows,
the holy God of endless days.

Sunday between 3 and 9 July inclusive

Proper 9

46 10 10 11 11

1. O let us rejoice and welcome our King,
triumphant he comes, true justice to bring.
No warhorse or chariot, no weapons or
pride,
but humbly he chooses a donkey to ride!

2. O let us rejoice in Christ, who can save
from selfish desires that seek to enslave:
temptations around us and conflicts within,
he triumphs for us in the struggle with sin.

3. O let us rejoice this myst'ry to know,
which God in his love has chosen to show.
Unspeakable wonder, unreachable prize,
his gift to his children, yet veiled from the
wise!

Sunday between 10 and 16 July inclusive

Proper 10

47 DCM

1. The word of God is sown like seed,
upon the waiting land,
and life-renewing water flows
from God's attentive hand.
His word can never fruitless be,
his purpose will succeed,
for grace abundant will fulfil
the deepest human need.

2. The seed of life is freely spent
on good and barren ground,
and in the plenitude of grace
the harvest will abound.
In justice and in liberty,
the Lord will show his face,
revealing his abundant love
to all the human race.

3. The seed of perfect life was sown
   to meet our deepest need,
   in Christ who bore our mortal sins
   with perfect grace indeed.
   His own life-giving Spirit brings
   fulfilment to the law,
   and raises us, once dead in sin,
   to life for evermore.

Sunday between 17 and 23 July inclusive

Proper 11

48 87 87

1. To you, O Lord, our only help,
   our life in love upholding,
   we bring a willing sacrifice,
   our constant praise unfolding;

2. For you alone are Lord Most High,
   in light eternal living,
   and from the greatness of your power
   a gentle judgement giving.

3. O Holy Spirit, love divine,
   our halting tongues enlighten,
   and by your wordless sighs of grace
   our sense of glory heighten.

4. O Holy Reaper, come with grace
   to us, whose hearts adore you,
   who long to see your kingdom come
   and stand in joy before you.

Sunday between 24 and 30 July inclusive

Proper 12

49 76 76 and refrain

God is in his holy place,
his reign shall never cease.
He will give the poor a home
and bring his people peace.

1. To him for countless ages
   have kings and beggars prayed
   for faith and perfect wisdom
   which cannot fail and fade.

2. He works with those who love him
   to see his purpose done,
   in faithful hearts perfecting
   the image of the Son.

3. This priceless pearl we long for:
   the faith that sets us free,
   to call both Lord and Brother
   the Christ of Calvary!

Sunday between 31 July and 6 August inclusive

Proper 13

50 88 88 88

1. O God of hope, your people hear;
   give peace to all who hurt or fear,
   with help and comfort ever near.

2. O you who give, with open hand,
   the produce of the sea and land,
   be bread for us who waiting stand.

3. You sent the Christ, with saving grace,
   to glorify your chosen race,
   open your truth and show your face.

4. In him your covenant was sealed,
   your word fulfilled, your grace revealed,
   your world made whole, the nations healed.

5. In lonely places long ignored,
   we hear your voice, O serving Lord:
   'Give them the food that I afford.'

6. Then let us see the hungry fed,
   with truth and justice, wine and bread,
   and honour Christ, our living head.

Sunday between 7 and 13 August inclusive

Proper 14

51 76 76 D

1. O God of grace and mercy,
your covenant is sure:
despite our mortal failings,
your promise will endure.
Come not in fire or earthquake,
or sign of worldly power,
but let your gentle whisper
announce the hallowed hour!

2. When storms of life around us
condemn our hearts to fear,
then let the voice of stillness
compose the anxious ear,
and from our fears remake us
with faithful hearts and brave,
who, fixing on the Saviour,
may ride the threat'ning wave.

3. O give us grace to follow
where Christ himself has trod,
in faith and hope proclaiming
the saving word of God:
the promise of redemption
availed to ev'ry race,
rests not on laws and sanctions,
but God's free gift of grace.

Sunday between 14 and 20 August inclusive

Proper 15

52 CM

1. O let the peoples praise you, Lord,
and let your way be known,
your saving pow'r upon the earth
in grace and judgement shown.

2. You call for justice and for truth
from all who bear your name;
your perfect grace is known of old,
and ever stays the same.

3. Your gifts can never be revoked,
your promise ever stands,
and disobedient hearts receive
great mercy at your hands.

4. Then shall your all-sufficient grace
throughout the world be spread,
and all creation come to share
your children's special bread.

Sunday between 21 and 27 August inclusive

Proper 16

53 10 10 11 11

1. Great Father of light, in glory above,
your promise reveals the pow'r of your love.
Your justice will brighten each nation and race,
and all your creation be ruled by your grace.

2. The fullness of grace in Jesus we see,
who humbled himself to set people free.
The keys of the kingdom to Peter he gave,
with pow'r and dominion to heal and to save.

3. By grace we are called, transformed and made new,
with pow'r to discern the good and the true,
with gifts in abundance to use in his name,
to give with compassion, to teach and proclaim.

4. The God who is known as One and as Three
commissions his church, his image to be:
though members are many, the body is one
that by our communion his will may be done.

Sunday between 28 August and 3 September inclusive

Proper 17

54 87 87 87

1. God of prophecy and promise,
   give us grace to bear your name;
   in the face of structured evil
   let us fearlessly proclaim:
   God is faithful to his people,
   God from age to age the same.

2. Let us not, for easy ransom,
   seek a cheaper price to pay;
   nor by faithless good intention
   bar the suff'ring Saviour's way.
   Lead us through the night of sorrow
   into glad salvation's day.

3. Grant us, in our life and worship,
   you alone to glorify;
   not afraid of truly living,
   nor, for you, afraid to die.
   When the world, for fear, rejects us,
   'Alleluia!' may we cry!

Sunday between 4 and 10 September inclusive

Proper 18

55 CM

1. O God of justice, righteous judge,
   what light your word imparts!
   Give us a clear prophetic voice
   and ever-gentle hearts.

2. May we on your transforming word
   our hearts for ever set;
   let peace our obligation be,
   and love our only debt.

3. May we, throughout our common life,
   the love of Christ reveal,
   by speaking truth in charity,
   and all our conflicts heal.

4. Then to the holy triune God
   let perfect praise ascend,
   when all the nations, bound in peace,
   bring conflict to an end.

Sunday between 11 and 17 September inclusive

Proper 19

56 SM

1. O gracious, faithful God,
   move swiftly to forgive,
   and in true love and fellowship
   let all your servants live.

2. Give us forgiving hearts
   when others' rage we know,
   and let us not fan anger's flames
   but costly mercy show.

3. Of countless debts forgiv'n,
   such mercies we receive;
   but others' paltry debts recall,
   and make the Saviour grieve.

4. O high eternal Lord,
   who shared our mortal shame,
   the living and the dead shall own
   your all-redeeming name.

Sunday between 18 and 24 September inclusive

Proper 20

57 DSM

1. Look to the Lord of life,
   and seek his way to learn;
   abandon every harmful thought
   and from all evil turn.
   O wonder unrevealed,
   so far our thoughts above,
   as far from us as heav'n from earth,
   his perfect way of love!

continued

2. Here may we live by grace,
from works' obsession freed,
and reckon not with wages earned
but only human need.
It is his sov'reign right
his mercies to bestow,
with justice ever more profound
than mortal mind can know.

3. O, for the life above
incessantly we long;
a life of unremitting joy
and sweet angelic song.
Yet deeper thought demands
we call this world our home,
and share in all its joys and woes
until his kingdom come.

Sunday between 25 September and 1 October inclusive

Proper 21

58 11 12 12 10

1. God of truth and justice, seated in splendour,
freely we confess that our hearts have disobeyed.
Father all-forgiving, merciful and tender,
favour your people, let your hand be stayed.

2. O with wonder hear it: word all astounding!
Now to saints and sinners is heav'n thrown open wide!
See the risen Saviour, grace and truth abounding,
welcome the people others have denied.

3. Christ from highest heaven, humbly descending,
chose to set his glory and majesty aside;
death in death defeating, hell's dominion ending,
then by the Father fully glorified!

4. So shall every nation, kneeling before him,
full of truth and beauty the Christ in glory see;
every tongue confess him, every heart adore him,
splendid in grace and endless mystery!

Sunday between 2 and 8 October inclusive

Proper 22

59 11 11 10 11

1. God, the great Creator, sets the world in place,
tenderly creating works of love and grace.
Father of beauty, everything you own,
earth and stars and heaven are your royal throne.

2. Like a fertile vineyard, tilled with loving care,
fruits of truth and justice should have flourished there.
O shame indeed: when came the reaping hour,
though with passion tended, every fruit was sour.

3. So our heav'nly Father sent his royal Son,
into his creation, trusting grace alone.
Faithful to death, he poured the blood divine,
made the vineyard ready for a sweeter wine!

4. Let us share your passion, Christ who shared our strife,
finding, through your suff'ring, resurrection life.
Hold us and make us evermore your own,
then in mercy bring us to your royal throne.

Sunday between 9 and 15 October inclusive

Proper 23

60 76 76 and refrain

God is longing to forgive
the sins we cannot face.
In his love we all may live,
O perfect work of grace!

1. Upon his holy mountain
a banquet he prepares,
removes all bitter poison
and life eternal shares.

2. Those chosen and invited
disdainfully decline,
so to the poor and humble
goes out the call divine!

3. And O what peace eternal,
in grace, he offers still:
through prayer and supplication,
our needs he will fulfil!

Sunday between 16 and 22 October inclusive

Proper 24

61 CM

1. O God, through all the nations' life,
in truth and justice move,
and breathe into the world's affairs
the politics of love.

2. When warring nations, in their fear,
the voice of hatred raise,
you work though unexpected hearts,
in unexpected ways!

3. Let not our worldly politics
ungraced and Godless be,
but in the coinage of our lives
your image may we see.

4. To God the Father, glory be,
through Christ the risen Lord,
whose Spirit breathes in all our prayers
the power of the Word!

Sunday between 23 and 29 October inclusive

Proper 25

62 76 76 D

1. God calls us to be holy,
as holy is his name,
obedient to his statutes,
and free from fear of blame;
to show no fear or favour,
seek not revenge or strife,
but truly love our neighbour
the way we love our life.

2. This is the great commandment
he gives to humankind:
to love our God completely,
with heart and soul and mind,
to seek our neighbour's welfare
the way we seek our own;
for in these two commandments
God's perfect way is shown.

3. So, in our life together,
this gospel we proclaim,
not seeking praise or payment,
or passing worldly fame,
but with the gospel message
our very selves we share,
and, by our gentle presence,
for others' needs we care.

4. God make us truly holy,
as we are called to be,
in sharing his compassion
for all humanity.
The worthy Son of David
ascends his Father's throne,
to rule in perfect justice
by pow'r of love alone.

All Saints' Day

63 DSM

1. Firm in the faith of God
   the saints have lived and died,
   who with the Son in glory stand,
   redeemed and purified.
   This is the glorious hope
   in which our hearts abound,
   to look upon the face of God
   with love eternal crowned.

2. Blessed are those who thirst
   for freedom, love and peace,
   who long to see the truth prevail
   and all injustice cease.
   The humble and the poor,
   and those who weep or mourn,
   shall rise with all the saints to see
   the new creation's dawn.

3. Children and heirs of God,
   oh, what a gift of grace,
   to be his children here and now,
   in mortal time and space!
   What we could yet become
   is yet to be made known,
   but in the fullness of his love
   his glory will be shown.

The Fourth Sunday before Advent

64 SM

1. Great Father of us all,
   come to our help we pray;
   recall us to your holy word
   and keep us in your way.

2. Let us not place our trust
   in temples built with stone,
   for in the faithful human heart
   is greater glory shown.

3. A greater glory this,
   and our much higher throne:
   to serve with such a humble love
   as his whose name we own.

4. Great Father of us all,
   your word we would obey.
   We glorify your holy name,
   and seek your perfect way.

The Third Sunday before Advent

65 DSM

1. Wisdom is ever bright,
   the light by which we see,
   revealed to our expectant sight,
   the depths of mystery!
   She graciously appears
   to all who seek her face,
   and calls us from our doubts and fears
   to know her life of grace.

2. Now in the waiting night,
   O let us watchful be,
   preparing for the blessed sight
   of Wisdom full and free;
   then let our lamps be bright,
   and hearts expectant burn,
   until, in uncreated light,
   the bridegroom shall return.

3. Joy of the aching heart,
   O bliss beyond compare;
   that those whom death now keeps apart
   that glorious day will share!
   O for the angel's voice,
   the trumpet's ringing sound,
   when all the saints in light rejoice
   in myst'ry so profound!

The Second Sunday before Advent

66 11 12 12 10

1. God of dreadful justice, come with salvation,
call us to account for the way your gifts are used:
judge the world's oppression, greed and exploitation
wealth meant for sharing, selfishly abused.

2. Master, all-perceiving, our weakness knowing,
yet to us entrusting resources rich and rare,
O return in glory, grace and love bestowing,
call us your kingdom's promises to share.

3. We in faith await you, humbly adoring,
moving from the darkness to resurrection's light,
'til the day appointed when, all life restoring,
Christ's perfect peace will all the world unite!

Christ the King:
The Sunday next before Advent

67 10 11 11 11 and refrain

1. Lord Christ, triumphant, universal King,
let redeemed creation celebrate and sing!
Seek the lost and scattered, lead the wand'rers home,
then in truth and wholeness, let your kingdom come!

Lord Christ, triumphant, universal King,
let redeemed creation celebrate and sing!

2. O perfect judgement, long-awaited grace,
justice and atonement for the human race!
Those who recognised you in the last and least,
now you call to join you in the kingdom's feast.

3. Spirit of wisdom, give us grace to see
Jesus in the glory of the Trinity,
risen and exalted by the Father's pow'r,
and, for all creation, bringing hope to flow'r.

Year B

The First Sunday of Advent

68 67 67 66 66

1. Return, Redeemer God,
   with judgement and with healing:
   restore our wayward hearts,
   your light and truth revealing.
   O leave us not alone,
   nor let us go astray,
   but open every heart
   to know your perfect way.

2. Here let us wait and pray
   to greet the Lord returning,
   as watchers in the night
   with beacons ever burning:
   for none can know the hour
   his people long to see,
   when Christ, in glory, comes
   to set creation free.

3. May grace and peace be ours,
   from God the Father flowing,
   through Jesus Christ, our Lord,
   his perfect truth bestowing.
   This Fellowship we share,
   the Father and the Son,
   who with the Spirit, Three,
   eternally are One.

The Second Sunday of Advent

69 11 12 12 10

1. Hark a voice is calling, clear and
   triumphant:
   'Make, across the desert, a highway for the
   Lord.
   Every hill and valley, level out before him:
   God comes in glory – hear his holy word!'

2. Gospel of redemption, word of forgiveness!
   God, in endless mercy, his people has
   restored.
   Sanctified by water, hallowed by the Spirit,
   life in abundance, Christ on us has poured!

3. God so long awaited, righteous in
   judgement,
   all creation trembles to see your holy face.
   Come in grace and glory, rule with truth
   and justice,
   holding creation in your love's embrace.

The Third Sunday of Advent

70 CM

1. Sing and rejoice, the Lord is near;
   his saving grace proclaim,
   and let the whole creation show
   the glory of his name.

2. We, by the Spirit's power, proclaim
   good news for all the poor:
   our God will set the captive free
   and tears shall be no more.

3. Here in the light of Christ alone,
   redeemed by grace, we stand,
   and treasure ev'ry perfect gift
   of his unfailing hand.

4. Freedom and truth, like garden flowers,
   upon the earth shall grow,
   and all the nations, lost in praise,
   his perfect peace will know.

The Fourth Sunday of Advent

71 76 76 D

1. The Saviour of the nations is born of
   David's line,
   from humble service lifted to majesty
   divine.
   He comes with peace and justice, in
   judgement ever sure;
   and, founded on compassion, his reign
   shall be secure.

continued

2. The Spirit is rejoicing in bringing hope to birth,
and life in all its fullness he breathes upon the earth.
Among the poor and lowly, his promise is received:
the Virgin's womb has flowered, the barren have conceived!

3. The myst'ry of the ages, the secret long-concealed,
of full and free salvation, at last has been revealed.
The Father's name we honour, through Jesus Christ, our Lord,
who, in the Spirit's power will ever be adored.

Christmas Day: Set 1

72 87 87 87

1. Those who walked in deepest darkness,
see at last a splendid light,
heralding a Son now given,
born of God to human sight.
He will reign in peace for ever,
setting every wrong to right.

2. Shepherds hear the angels calling,
telling of a newborn King
lying in a straw-filled manger;
O, the awesome song they sing!
'Glory in the highest heaven!'
All the world with joy will ring!

3. Now, the work of grace completed,
all creation reconciled,
let us live in Godly freedom,
not as slaves by sin defiled;
seek again the greater glory
once revealed in Mary's child.

Christmas Day: Set 2

73 10 10 10 10

1. Proclaim good news, God's people have been saved,
this day salvation dawns upon the earth.
Build up, build up the highway for the Lord,
proclaim God's majesty, and human worth!

2. Proclaim good news: new life is flowing free,
not by our goodness but by God's own grace,
through Jesus Christ, our Saviour and our Lord:
he pours his Spirit into every place.

3. Proclaim good news: great joy to all the world,
to us is born a Saviour, Christ the Lord.
'Glory to God!' the angel host proclaim.
'And peace on earth!' we cry with one accord.

Christmas Day: Set 3

74 87 87 87

1. Lovely feet upon the mountains
bring the distant runner near,
with the word of true salvation,
set to gladden every ear.
Sing for joy, you ransomed people,
God has made the vision clear.

2. Now in even greater glory
comes the co-eternal Word,
he through whom, in primal darkness,
first creation's breath was stirred.
All the glory of the Godhead
in his form is seen and heard.

3. He, the Father's very image,
   came to save and justify,
   then, the full atonement finished,
   took his proper place on high.
   Now his name, with awe and wonder,
   all the angels glorify.

The First Sunday of Christmas

75 67 67 66 66

1. O come, incarnate God,
   with garments of salvation,
   let righteousness and peace
   spring up in every nation.
   We long to hear your voice,
   so see salvation's flame,
   and call the world to know
   the glory of your name.

2. With Mary, now we stand
   in gracious awe and wonder,
   this great mysterious word
   to treasure and to ponder;
   the word of perfect grace
   by simple shepherds told,
   yet ever more profound
   than scholar's mind can hold!

3. O Abba! Father! God!
   Your children seek your blessing,
   who stand before your throne,
   imperfect praise expressing.
   O bless us with your peace,
   preserve us by your grace,
   and let us here behold
   the radiance of your face!

The Second Sunday of Christmas

76 84 84 88 84

1. Word made flesh, eternal Wisdom
   born from above,
   light and life of all creation,
   perfect in love;
   faithful to the Father's sending,
   perfectly our nature blending
   by the Spirit's power, attending
   as holy Dove.

2. Come to call your faithful people
   from ev'ry place,
   come to make our hearts your temple,
   radiant with grace;
   come, the Father's love revealing,
   to our wayward souls appealing,
   'til, within his presence kneeling,
   we see his face.

3. Blessèd be our God and Father,
   Saviour and Lord,
   calling us to be his children
   still by his Word,
   who before the world's foundation
   planned our undeserved salvation;
   hail him God of all creation,
   ever adored!

The Epiphany

77 86 88 6

1. Arise to greet the Lord of light,
   you people of his choice.
   In uncreated glory bright,
   he bursts upon our inward sight,
   and bids the heart rejoice! *(2)*

2. Towards his light shall kings be drawn
   this majesty to see,
   and in the brightness of the dawn,
   shall see the longing world reborn
   in justice full and free. *(2)*

continued

3. The holy light in Judah's skies
calls sages from afar.
Great minds in meek obedience rise,
and call the world to recognise
creation's guiding star! *(2)*

4. This majesty for long concealed
from longing human sight,
in Jesus Christ is now revealed,
and God's eternal promise sealed
in love's unending light. *(2)*

The Baptism of Christ

78 87 87 87

1. God who breathed, in the beginning,
on the dark and formless deep,
with the Word that called creation
out of its primeval sleep.
Alleluia! Alleluia!
At your word, our spirits leap!

2. In the fullness of your purpose
was the Word in flesh revealed,
with authority of heaven
in the Holy Spirit sealed.
Alleluia! Alleluia!
Here our souls are fully healed.

3. Father, breathe that Word upon us
in the waters of rebirth,
with transforming pow'r uniting
Godly grace and human worth.
Alleluia! Alleluia!
Pour your Spirit on the earth!

The Second Sunday of Epiphany

79 LM

1. The call of God, in ancient times,
was by the youthful prophet heard,
who opened up both ear and heart
to hear the life-disrupting word.

2. The first disciples heard the call
to share the risk of faith and prayer,
and left their old familiar ways
to follow Christ, they knew not where.

3. God give us faith, with them, to see
the meeting-point of heav'n and earth,
and witness, at the journey's end,
the joyful new creation's birth.

4. Then shall the Lion upon the throne,
unseal at last the sacred scroll,
when he, the sacrificial lamb
has truly made creation whole.

The Third Sunday of Epiphany

80 87 87 87

1. Blessèd be the God of Abram,
full of majesty divine!
In your faithful priests and people,
may your glory ever shine.
Here we celebrate your goodness,
breaking bread and sharing wine.

2. In the life of all the nations,
let us see this wondrous sign:
water too impure for drinking
you can turn to holy wine!
O the splendour, O the glory!
Truth and justice here will shine.

3. Blessed are the ones invited
to the Lamb's great marriage feast,
where the praises of the righteous,
like a flood, will be released
in unending alleluias,
age by glorious age increased.

The Fourth Sunday of Epiphany

81 11 11 10 11

1. God has raised a prophet from among our own,
who, in word and action, perfect truth has shown;
speaking in judgement, yet the voice of grace,
hope eternal springing, here in time and space!

2. Christ as you empower us, let us clearly speak,
hush the voice of evil and uphold the weak;
end all oppression, set the captives free,
'til the world rejoices grace and truth to see.

3. Grace and truth will triumph, evil schemes will fail,
in the face of terror, goodness will prevail.
Christ, by your presence, give our souls release,
trusting in the promise of your reign of peace.

The Presentation of Christ in the Temple

82 87 87 D

1. Oh, the wonder of the ages,
God is held in mortal hands,
offered in an earthly temple
to fulfil the law's demands!
With what grace, immortal Being
shares our flesh and draws our breath,
by his life true life imparting,
by his death, destroying death.

2. Lord, transform our earthly temples
with your covenant of grace,
make us ready for your coming,
fit to stand before your face.
By your own refining presence,
come to purify and bless,
that our lives may be an off'ring
full of truth and righteousness.

3. Come, then, Lord, in grace and judgement,
shaming all our greed and pride,
to the broken and exploited,
all the world has cast aside.
Come, your very self to offer
to the greatest and the least,
then present us to the Father,
Christ, our brother, Saviour, Priest.

Sunday between 3 and 9 February inclusive
(if earlier than the Second Sunday before Lent)

Proper 1

83 76 76 and refrain

'Freedom! Freedom!' let us cry
for all who are oppressed.
'Freedom!' cries the God of hope
from furthest east and west.

1. For those whose life is joyless,
whose spirits know despair,
whose rights are disregarded,
God calls on us to care.

2. For those confined by illness,
or gripped by guilt or fear,
whose cries, though here unheeded,
have reached the Saviour's ear:

3. For those obsessed with duties,
or seeking for rewards,
who lose the joy and freedom
which selfless love affords:

Sunday between 10 and 16 February inclusive
(if earlier than the Second Sunday before Lent)

Proper 2

84 55 54 D

1. God of salvation, cleanse us and cure us,
come, reassure us, speaking in grace,
prejudice healing, goodness revealing,
holding creation in your embrace.

continued

2. Humble in glory, healing and holding,
warmly enfolding all we would spurn,
you recreate them, and reinstate them,
sharing the story, helping us learn.

3. Onward you lead us, loving and learning,
longing and yearning your prize to gain:
boundless compassion, grace without ration,
for love you freed us, in love you reign.

Sunday between 17 and 23 February inclusive
(if earlier than the Second Sunday before Lent)

Proper 3

85 LM

1. O holy God, forgive our sins,
and let us not the past recall;
you open up the way of hope,
renewing life within us all.

2. We bring you our disabling fears,
our sightless eyes, our narrow mind,
and, in the presence of your Word,
a greater strength and vision find.

3. Your holy word we now proclaim;
the promises in Christ revealed,
remembered here in bread and wine,
and in the Holy Spirit sealed.

4. In you our only hope is found,
and so we come before your face,
to sing your everlasting praise,
and glory in your perfect grace.

The Second Sunday before Lent

86 87 87 D

1. Wisdom of the God of heaven,
present at creation's birth,
long before he shaped the mountains,
poured the seas or formed the earth;
may we treasure understanding,
as a special gift of grace,
but – the highest form of wisdom –
may we love the human race.

2. Christ, the firstborn of creation,
image of the God of light,
by whose pow'r, from primal darkness,
heav'n and earth were brought to sight:
first on earth, and first in heaven,
first from death itself reborn,
shine in all your radiant splendour
at the new creation's dawn.

3. Word, with God in the beginning,
Word of God, and God indeed,
holy Wisdom made incarnate
for creation's deepest need.
To your own, though once rejected,
come again in truth and grace,
bringing uncreated glory
into mortal time and space.

The Sunday Next before Lent

87 87 87 D

1. All the glory of the Godhead
is revealed to mortal sight,
yet the flesh that manifests it
serves to veil the dazzling light.
Once the words of law and prophets
sought to make that glory known,
now the Word, upon the mountain,
makes our mortal flesh his throne!

2. Glory of the Father's image,
shining in the living Word,
in the gospel's proclamation
may be fully seen and heard.
Let us not, for worldly blindness,
veil our senses from its light,
Christ himself, from deepest darkness,
shines with hope and glory bright.

3. As Elijah, on the whirlwind,
was removed from mortal sight,
so the glory of the heavens
veils the living Word in light;
yet his Spirit, in abundance,
on his servant church is poured,
lighting all our darkest places
with glory of the Lord.

Ash Wednesday

88 87 87 D

1. Holy God, of righteous glory,
see your people gathered here,
in a solemn congregation,
your forgiving word to hear.
God of love and slow to anger,
gracious, longing to restore,
hear your priests and people calling,
give us grace to sin no more.

2. We confess the pride we suffer,
needs which none can satisfy;
how we love the praise of mortals,
swift to flow'r and quick to die.
Let us find rewards eternal
as we quietly seek your face,
and our open, public living
witness only to your grace.

3. Free us from our self-bound living,
better witnesses to be
to the world by grace appealing,
telling forth the mystery:
how creation's pure Redeemer
walked among us undefiled,
by his deathless love proclaiming,
God with us is reconciled.

The First Sunday of Lent

89 86 88 6

1. O God of truth, your dreadful might,
in judgement's flood was shown;
yet to our undeserving sight,
in gracious arcs of dancing light,
your promises are known.

2. By light and water, still you bring
your people to your side,
who drink from hope's eternal Spring,
and joyful songs of freedom sing
with Christ, now glorified.

3. The way of truth shall be our choice,
with all its doubt and fear;
let us not heed the tempter's voice,
but in the gospel word rejoice:
'Behold the kingdom near!'

The Second Sunday of Lent

90 10 10 11 11

1. Remember, O God, your promise of old;
which Abram, through faith, was worthy
to hold.
Your covenant stands as a witness to grace,
a blessing and sign to each nation and race.

2. Incarnate, you sought the broken and lost,
not shirking the pain, nor counting the cost.
You call us this work of salvation to share,
and find perfect life at the heart of despair.

3. Your promise depends on faith in your
grace,
not keeping the law or winning the race.
In faith let us follow where Jesus has led,
and trust in the God who brought life
from the dead.

The Third Sunday of Lent

91 LM

1. The wisdom of the living God
is seen in Jesus crucified;
such weakness can unite and heal
where human pow'r and strength divide.

2. The ancient books contain the law
of love for God and humankind;
the Word incarnate lives and breathes
with grace and mercy unconfined!

3. Both grace and judgement here are found,
his body is the perfect sign:
though once destroyed by human hands,
now raised, and filled with life divine.

continued

4. Redeemer God, O give us grace
 to find new life in one who died,
 and call the world to rise and share
 the wisdom of the Crucified.

4. May Mary's faith be found
 in ev'ry human heart,
 to wonder at the mystery
 and play our humble part.

The Fourth Sunday of Lent

92 SM

1. From death to life restored,
 from sin to hope reborn,
 God leads us on the desert way
 toward salvation's dawn.

2. God's work of art we are,
 in Christ for wholeness made,
 though dead in sin, now brought to life
 by grace and mercy saved.

3. For God so loved the world
 that Christ, incarnate, came,
 confronting evil, fear and death
 with love's eternal name.

4. Then let the world rejoice
 to see salvation's dawn,
 when all creation is at peace,
 by grace and faith reborn.

Mothering Sunday

93 SM

1. O God of perfect love,
 your promises we own,
 that through a mother's tender care
 your glory can be shown.

2. Then give us faith to know
 your word will never fail:
 the troubles of the present day
 a brighter future veil.

3. The temple prophet speaks,
 and we his vision see,
 of pain and blessings both to come
 in every family.

The Fifth Sunday of Lent

94 87 87 D

1. See, the promised time is coming,
 when the covenant of grace,
 in unbroken truth and freedom
 will this longing world embrace.
 Then shall God be known and
 worshipped
 by the greatest and the least,
 in the light of perfect justice,
 at the royal kingdom's feast.

2. To a life of prayer and passion,
 Christ, the Word eternal came;
 found perfection in obedience,
 and received the highest name.
 Author of the world's salvation,
 teach us humbly to obey,
 sharing in the pain and sorrow
 of redemption's costly way.

3. Saviour Christ, eternal Victim,
 seed of hope who fell and died,
 by our sacrificial living
 may the church be glorified.
 Let our lives be freely scattered
 in the dark, oppressive ground,
 'til the day when truth and wholeness,
 God's great harvest, will abound.

Palm Sunday: Liturgy of the Passion

95 SM

1. What dreadful sight is this,
 by fear and envy wrought,
 the faithful servant of the Lord
 in pain and death distraught!

2. But God will give him strength,
with patience to endure,
and bring him through this time of trial
in word and action pure.

3. And now, before our eyes,
a myst'ry so divine;
redemption's wondrous story, told
in broken bread and wine!

4. The co-eternal Son,
in splendour bright arrayed,
for us his glory set aside
and unto death obeyed.

5. Exalted over all,
and giv'n the highest name,
him shall all nations, kings and pow'rs
eternally acclaim.

Maundy Thursday

96 14 14 4 7 8

1. God of the Passover, Author and Lord
of salvation,
gladly we gather to bring you our hearts'
adoration;
ransomed and free,
called and commissioned to be
signs of your love for creation.

2. Here we remember that evening of
wonder enthralling,
myst'ry of passion divine, and betrayal
appalling.
Breaking the bread,
'This is my body,' he said.
'Do this, my passion recalling.'

3. God of the Eucharist, humbly we gather
before you,
and, at your table, for pardon and grace
we implore you.
Under the cross,
counting as profit our loss,
deep in its shade, we adore you.

Good Friday

97 84 84 88 84

1. Day of wrath and day of wonder,
whence hope has fled!
See the body torn asunder,
blood freely shed.
Stripped of majesty we saw him,
human sight recoiled before him,
yet it was our sorrows tore him;
for us he bled.

2. Day of hope and day of glory,
though unperceived!
See redemption's dreadful story,
long, long conceived.
Evil pow'rs, in tatters lying,
knowing death itself is dying,
hear the voice triumphant crying,
'All is achieved!'

3. Day of majesty and splendour,
here ends the race!
Christ, our Priest, our souls' defender,
longs to embrace.
He who walked this earth before us,
tried and tempted, yet victorious,
calls us to the kingdom glorious.
O, perfect grace!

Easter Day

98 CM or 86 86 extended

1. To him who died is now restored
the life he freely gave.
We worship here the Lord of life,
now risen, risen risen,
risen from the grave!

2. The misty light of early dawn
reveals an empty cave.
How vain to search the tomb for one
now risen, risen, risen,
risen from the grave!

continued

3. His were the hands that healed the sick,
   and made the fearful brave.
   Though once despised, his power we sec
   now risen, risen, risen,
   risen from the grave!

4. The pleasures of this passing age
   cannot our souls enslave;
   for true contentment rests with him,
   now risen, risen, risen,
   risen from the grave!

5. To all creation, we proclaim,
   'The pow'r to heal and save
   is vested in the living Lord
   now risen, risen, risen,
   risen from the grave!'

The Second Sunday of Easter

99 98 98

1. 'We have not seen the risen Saviour
   in flesh and blood, before our eyes!'
   The frailty of our mortal senses
   for proof, unveiled and certain, cries.

2. But we have heard the proclamation,
   the call from darkness into light,
   to share the life of faith and service
   that brings the living Lord to sight.

3. The risen Christ we now acknowledge,
   who meets us here in bread and wine,
   and calls us into close communion
   to share the fellowship divine.

4. He calls us now to recognise him
   in those whose worth the world denies,
   so may we see the risen Saviour
   in flesh and blood before our eyes!

The Third Sunday of Easter

100 DCM

1. The 'justice' of this fallen world,
   in all its shame we see,
   when innocents are crucified
   to keep the brutal free.
   But greater is the God of truth,
   who raised the One who died,
   and calls us all to life and hope
   in Christ, now glorified.

2. He shows his wounded hands and feet
   to all who live in fear,
   and both in word and sacrament
   reveals the kingdom near.
   And still, in places dark with death,
   he calls us to his side
   as witnesses of living hope
   to people crucified.

3. The justice of our Father's love
   is shown in truth and grace,
   by which alone, his children hope
   to look upon his face.
   Yet what, by grace, we may become
   for now remains concealed,
   until in awesome purity
   God's glory is revealed.

The Fourth Sunday of Easter

101 CM

1. The love of God in Jesus Christ
   is gloriously made known,
   yet not in words but kindly acts
   its fullness will be shown.

2. He came to earth with living power
   to heal and to restore;
   his name brings healing, strength and hope,
   and justice to the poor.

3. As children of the living God,
   we stand within this place,
   by love redeemed, yet still to learn
   the full extent of grace.

4. Then praise the God of perfect love,
   who longs to save the lost;
   and praise the Shepherd who reveals
   the glory and the cost.

The Fifth Sunday of Easter

102 76 76 and refrain

Sing a new and joyful song
to God who makes us one;
he the nations' hope reveals
by pow'r of love alone.

1. God's presence is around us,
   and yet we have no fear;
   we find no accusation,
   nor condemnation here.

2. On Christ alone depending
   the life divine we share,
   and fruits of peace and justice
   the healthy vine will bear.

3. God give us grace and courage
   this gospel to proclaim:
   the word of perfect freedom
   and justice, in his name.

The Sixth Sunday of Easter

103 DSM

1. Come, let us live by love
   which flows from God alone,
   whose life and truth in Christ we see,
   in radiant beauty shown.
   The Spirit gives us grace
   to follow where Christ trod,
   and know that everyone who loves
   is born and known of God.

2. God is the only source
   of love that knows no end;
   which, open to another's pain,
   itself will freely spend.
   This is the great command:
   to live within that love,
   until the world is filled with peace
   and glory from above.

3. Wake to the Spirit's voice,
   proclaiming from outside,
   'In unexpected people, still,
   will God be glorified,
   whose love embraces all,
   of every creed and race;
   so praise, with them, love's only Source,
   the God of truth and grace!'

Ascension Day

104 87 87 87

1. Hail the risen Christ, ascending
   to his holy Father's side;
   angels, lost in awe and wonder,
   now acclaim the Lord who died.
   Alleluia!
   Christ triumphant, glorified.

2. He who once, from royal splendour,
   came to share our state of blame,
   now ascends in clouds of glory
   to the heights from which he came.
   Alleluia!
   Christ for evermore the same!

3. He will grant his praying servants,
   from the riches of his pow'r,
   grace to life as risen people,
   in this present watching hour.
   Alleluia!
   God on us his blessings show'r.

continued

4. Now, he bids us tell his story,
 where the lost and fearful roam:
 he will come again in glory,
 and will lead his people home.
 Alleluia!
 Maranatha! Come, Lord, come.

The Seventh Sunday of Easter

105 10 11 11 12

1. God of all goodness, whose word we believe,
 O, help us your promise to hear and receive,
 that life in abundance is found in your Son,
 and, in him united, all your people are one.

2. Saviour, you call us new life to proclaim,
 announce resurrection and hope in your name;
 your spirit unites us as witnesses all,
 who live in your presence and respond to your call.

3. You we acknowledge, your love we have known;
 within you our spirits have quickened and grown.
 We share in your Spirit of freedom divine;
 let love and love only be our token and sign.

4. Call us, unite us and send us by grace
 the broken and guilty to heal and embrace;
 to love may we witness, with common accord,
 in truth consecrated, by the power of the word.

Day of Pentecost

106 CM Richmond

1. The Spirit of the living God
 upon the earth is poured,
 inspiring humankind with love
 God only can afford.

2. O Spirit, come to all who wait,
 in longing or in fear,
 and send us out to speak of hope
 in word and action clear.

3. You lead us from our darkest fears,
 and self-indulgent ways,
 to where the light of truth and peace
 upon our vision plays.

4. Great Advocate, in ways of truth
 our wand'ring spirits guide,
 and in the giving of our lives
 may God be glorified.

Trinity Sunday

107 10 11 11 11 and refrain

1. Lead us to freedom
 God of liberty;
 Father, Son and Spirit,
 holy One-in-Three,
 throned above the temple,
 robed in smoke and fear,
 purify your people,
 your great call to hear.

Lead us to freedom,
God of liberty;
Father, Son and Spirit,
holy One-in-Three.

2. We, by the Spirit,
 'Abba! Father!' cry;
 now to hope and freedom
 let us testify.
 Both in joy and sorrow,
 heirs, with Christ, of God,
 let us dare to follow
 where his feet have trod.

3. Christ, sent among us
   by the Father's love,
   breathe in us your Spirit,
   new life from above.
   Then let life abundant
   flow in every place,
   all the world exulting
   in your boundless grace.

Sunday between 29 May and 4 June inclusive
(if after Trinity Sunday)

Proper 4

108 DSM

1. God of redemptive power,
   you set your people free,
   and move us from oppression's death
   to life and liberty;
   this day you set aside,
   a sign of love's release,
   to call a world enslaved by greed
   to value rest and peace.

2. Word of eternal life,
   through streets and fields you trod,
   and, to the narrow, law-bound mind,
   revealed the way of God:
   no soul-enslaving law,
   but liberating grace
   to make, within our crowded lives,
   a light and open space.

3. Light of the waiting world,
   in darkest places shine,
   and open to our awe-struck hearts
   the mystery divine.
   These earthen vessels fill
   with over-flowing grace,
   'til all creation comes to rest
   in liberty's embrace.

Sunday between 5 and 11 June inclusive
(if after Trinity Sunday)

Proper 5

109 LM

1. O Source of goodness, truth and light,
   forgive us our unholy ways,
   and show us how to make our lives
   a fitting sacrifice of praise.

2. Help us to hear and recognise
   your word of healing for our shame,
   and not, through jealousy or fear,
   the very Word of life defame.

3. Our common hope and faith is found
   in you who raised the Crucified;
   then be your life within us shown
   and grace among us multiplied.

4. We praise you, great Creator God,
   in whose redeeming Word we see
   the fullness of the Spirit's power,
   the wholeness of the Trinity.

Sunday between 12 and 18 June inclusive
(if after Trinity Sunday)

Proper 6

110 87 87 87

1. See the kingdom grow and flourish
   from the smallest shoot or seed;
   on its spreading branches bearing
   fruit to meet creation's need.
   Here the destitute find shelter,
   sick are healed and captives freed.

2. Constantly, through light and darkness,
   will the fruitful kingdom grow,
   spreading peace and bearing justice,
   giving further seeds to sow;
   from the hand of God, abundant
   grace and goodness overflow.

continued

3. Let us now in perfect freedom
take our place within its shade,
looking forward to the promise
by this parable displayed,
when injustice shall be ended,
burdens lifted, debts repaid.

Sunday between 19 and 25 June inclusive (if after Trinity Sunday)

Proper 7

111 77 77 77

1. God of love, whose voice we hear
speaking at the heart of fear,
bidding rampant chaos cease,
bringing order, making peace;
love's amazing story tell,
and our selfish pride dispel.

2. Speak, to calm our anxious hearts,
with the peace your word imparts.
Let us for each other live,
and to fearful people give
rising hope for falling tears,
selfless love for selfish fears.

3. In injustice, fear or pain,
may your grace be not in vain,
but the faith that we profess
strengthen us in righteousness.
Let us ever watch and pray,
looking to salvation's day.

Sunday between 26 June and 2 July inclusive

Proper 8

112 87 87 87

1. God, the source of life eternal,
in whose image we are made,
in the goodness of creation
is your pow'r and love displayed.
Let us live the life of wholeness,
in your presence, unafraid.

2. Christ, enthroned in heav'nly splendour,
bless us by your poverty;
in the use of our possessions,
help us signs of grace to be.
Let us live the life of heaven,
glorious in simplicity!

3. Those who touch life's outer edges
to its heart are now restored
and, in place of dereliction,
life abundant has been poured;
where the pow'r of death oppresses,
breathe your liberating Word.

Sunday between 3 and 9 July inclusive

Proper 9

113 76 76 D

1. The Spirit breathes upon us,
and calls us all to stand
for faithfulness and justice,
in this rebellious land;
though openly rejected,
and stubbornly ignored,
we lay before the nations
the true prophetic word.

2. The carpenter we follow,
though not of noble birth,
with bleeding hands remodelled
the structures of the earth.
By those he loves rejected,
his Spirit never dies,
but calls the new creation
in glorious hope to rise.

3. His is the only power
we dare to recognise,
for in our human weakness
his great potential lies.
So let the church, rejoicing,
the world's contempt embrace,
with greater joy proclaiming
the saving power of grace.

Sunday between 10 and 16 July inclusive

Proper 10

114 11 11 10 11

1. Called from safer pastures, lifestyles of our choice,
challenging injustice with the prophet's voice,
firm may we stand, the message to proclaim,
when the world would send us back from whence we came!

2. When by worldly princes pow'r has been abused,
let your word of judgement never be confused:
stirred by your Spirit, boldly may we speak,
bring the strong to justice, recompense the weak.

3. Glory to the Father, and the holy Son,
by whose grace and passion is our freedom won;
Spirit of promise, pledge of things to be,
let the world sing 'Glory to the Trinity!'

Sunday between 17 and 23 July inclusive

Proper 11

115 87 87 D

1. Listen to the voice of judgement,
all who cause the poor to weep;
leaders who exploit the people,
shepherds who neglect the sheep;
God will call the lost and scattered,
give the silent poor a voice,
and in perfect truth and justice
all the powerless shall rejoice.

2. See the Word of grace and judgement,
to the world, in Christ, revealed;
those who hear, in faith responding,
find their broken spirits healed.
Here, the victims of oppression
learn of mercy, truth and peace;
death is faced with life abundant,
and the captives find release.

3. Christ, our reconciling Saviour,
all hostility destroy;
by the Spirit's gracious presence,
make us one in peace and joy.
Let us praise your triune glory,
great Creator, holy Word,
in the unifying Spirit
ever worshipped and adored!

Sunday between 24 and 30 July inclusive

Proper 12

116 87 87

1. In hopeful trust, O God, we come
to hear your promise spoken,
that you will give the poor a home,
and heal the lost and broken.

2. The harvest of the land and sea
to us is freely given,
and, in your outstretched, open hand,
portrays the feast of heaven.

3. O Christ, make every mortal heart
a fit and proper dwelling,
to show the breadth and depth of love,
beyond all human telling.

4. Then may our God be glorified,
in every generation,
his Spirit be our inner strength
and Christ our full salvation.

Sunday between 31 July and 6 August inclusive

Proper 13

117 87 87 47

1. Holy manna, bread of heaven,
   given by the God of grace;
   sign of life and hope eternal,
   in the world of time and space;
   in your presence, in your presence
   life and wholeness we embrace. *(2)*

2. Christ, the bread of life, once broken,
   be yourself our only sign;
   give us strength of mind and purpose
   for the work of love divine.
   By your Spirit, by your Spirit,
   meet us here in bread and wine. *(2)*

3. One the body, one the Spirit,
   one the hope that we embrace,
   one the bond of peace and wholeness,
   one baptismal act of grace.
   Christ our Saviour, Christ our Saviour,
   let us see you face to face.

Sunday between 7 and 13 August inclusive

Proper 14

118 SM

1. In every heart, O God,
   your covenant restore;
   arise in glorious life and hope,
   defender of the poor.

2. Hear all despairing souls,
   and see your people fed;
   sustain the broken and oppressed
   with eucharistic bread.

3. In Christ, the bread of life,
   rejected by his own,
   we see the highest work of grace
   the world has ever known.

4. O Holy Spirit, come,
   our selfishness remove,
   and make of all our broken lives
   a sacrifice of love.

Sunday between 14 and 20 August inclusive

Proper 15

119 87 87 87

1. Here, upon a holy table,
   Wisdom's banquet is prepared;
   at her call the bread is broken,
   wine is freely poured and shared.
   From our folly still she calls us;
   life and vision are her fare.

2. Here the Bread of life is broken,
   wine recalls the lifeblood shed,
   sign of hope from sorrow springing,
   life eternal from the dead.
   So mysterious, yet so simple,
   flowing wine and broken bread!

3. Spirit of the risen Saviour,
   call us now to Wisdom's feast;
   fill us with the joy of living,
   from our foolishness released.
   Then to God, through Christ, be offered
   thanks and praise that never cease.

Sunday between 21 and 27 August inclusive

Proper 16

120 87 87 D

1. God of life and God of freedom,
   lead your wand'ring people home;
   let our anxious hearts be strengthened
   and our idols overthrown.
   You alone can liberate us
   from the chains to which we cling;
   you alone the word have spoken
   whence eternal life will spring.

2. Word of life, our hearts disturbing,
calling us in faith to move
from our safe and selfish present,
through the wilderness of love;
may our sacrificial living
show how firmly we believe:
those who take the risk of dying
shall eternal life receive.

3. Spirit of our God, prepare us
for the struggles we must face:
not on strength of arms relying,
but on your abundant grace.
Gird us round with truth and justice,
let our feet with peace be shod,
and, in prayer and supplication,
seek the holy way of God.

Sunday between 28 August and 3 September inclusive

Proper 17

121 11 12 12 10

1. Holy and unchanging, God ever-faithful,
source of all perfection and uncreated light.
In the law, you give us truth and
understanding;
may our obedience bring your love to sight.

2. Not in words and tokens lies our obedience,
nor in our obsession with mere external
signs.
By your word, disturb us, challenge and
confront us;
let your compassion all our lives refine.

3. Give us true religion, hearing and active,
faithful in our service of all who are
oppressed;
'til, in hope rejoicing, humble are exalted,
captives are freed and all the poor are
blessed.

Sunday between 4 and 10 September inclusive

Proper 18

122 CM

1. 'Be not afraid, your God will come,'
we hear the prophet sing.
'And living waters, at his word,
shall from the desert spring!

2. 'Then shall the sightless people see,
the deaf rejoice to hear;
the voiceless poor shall sing for joy,
the lame shall leap like deer!'

3. Come then, O Christ, the Word of life,
our senses to befriend,
and to our opened ears proclaim
the love that has no end.

4. Then no distinction let us make
of gender, class or race,
but to the world, in hope, proclaim
the openness of grace.

Sunday between 11 and 17 September inclusive

Proper 19

123 LM

1. The servant of the living God
is found among the humble poor;
in their oppression he will share,
and human dignity restore.

2. The Servant now we recognise
as Son of man and Son of God;
then let us follow, not obstruct,
the painful path of hope he trod.

3. He calls us to a living faith,
a faith that seeks the holy way,
that lets the love of Christ alone
direct the things we do and say.

4. O give us grace, eternal God,
within the world to take our place,
and let our words and actions show
the presence of undying grace.

Sunday between 18 and 24 September inclusive

Proper 20

124 87 87 87

1. Human wisdom has no measure
   for the foolishness of grace:
   false ideas of pow'r and pleasure
   crucify the human race.
   Who would dare to voice a protest?
   Who would take the victim's case?

2. Higher Wisdom God can offer;
   Christ, in death, has power to save,
   loving both the saint and scoffer
   in the shadow of the grave!
   Let us, then, with childlike wonder,
   live the life he freely gave.

3. In a life of true compassion,
   let us work for hope and peace,
   showing love in costly action,
   bidding exploitation cease;
   constantly for wisdom praying,
   that the kingdom may increase.

4. Save us from all religious pride,
   and narrowness of mind,
   that we may recognise your love
   in all of humankind.

Sunday between 25 September and 1 October inclusive

Proper 21

125 CM

1. Help us, O God, to hear your word,
   your promises believe,
   as in the unexpected voice
   your challenge we receive.

2. Through voices we have never known,
   of unfamiliar name,
   in faith and culture far apart,
   your purpose you proclaim.

3. Open our hearts to hear your word
   of comfort in distress,
   the word that comes to test and heal,
   to challenge and to bless.

Sunday between 2 and 8 October inclusive

Proper 22

126 77 77 77

1. God, who man and woman made,
   that your love might be displayed,
   care be given to the earth,
   life and beauty brought to birth;
   cover all the human race
   with the glory of your grace.

2. Christ, in homes most humble found,
   and with highest glory crowned,
   come and fill each painful place
   with your all-perfecting grace;
   in our homes be glorified,
   and creation sanctified.

3. Christ, above the angels raised,
   by your ransomed people praised,
   you who once drew mortal breath,
   tasted mortal pain and death,
   bring us to the Father's side,
   healed, redeemed and purified.

Sunday between 9 and 15 October inclusive

Proper 23

127 11 11 11 11

1. The spirit of wisdom is brighter than gold;
   her riches and splendour no coffers can
   hold.
   So flawless her beauty, no wealth can
   compare;
   no sceptre so noble, no silver so rare!

2. The wisdom of God is the gospel of grace,
which all who love riches find hard to embrace.
His challenge to goodness let no one ignore,
to humble ourselves for the sake of the poor.

3. 'Seek good and not evil,' the prophet commands.
'In justice and mercy, fulfil God's demands!'
So, cast not the poor and the needy aside,
but push away, rather, our greed and our pride.

4. The secret desires of our hearts will be known,
when all that is hidden is opened and shown;
when all of the humble to glory are raised,
and God in creation eternally praised.

Sunday between 16 and 22 October inclusive

Proper 24

128 87 87

1. The Servant, crushed with pain, we see,
his body bruised and broken,
and yet his suff'ring will fulfil
the promise God has spoken.

2. His broken body yet reveals
the glory of salvation;
his humble majesty outshines
the leaders of the nations.

3. For earthly kings and queens are found
in regal splendour living,
but God reveals the perfect rule:
a life of humble giving.

4. In Christ, eternal life is shown,
who suffered our temptation,
but sinless rose our great high priest,
redeeming all creation.

Sunday between 23 and 29 October inclusive

Proper 25

129 686 66 and refrain

1. Sing for joy, all the earth,
God has brought hope to birth,
and affirms human worth,
liberation bringing,
songs of freedom singing!

Come and worship God,
come and worship God,
life and light,
health and sight,
justice overflowing!

2. Jesus calls us to see
what a world this could be,
full of truth, just and free,
life abundant knowing,
into wholeness growing.

3. Christ, our priest, goes before,
life and hope to restore;
let the world all adore,
and the whole creation
hear the invitation:

All Saints' Day

130 DSM

1. Joy of the saints at rest,
the festival divine,
a feast of rich abundant food
and clear, well-mellowed wine.
Our God will wipe away
the tears from every face,
and aching hearts rejoice to taste
his long-awaited grace.

continued

2. This is the mountaintop
where all the tribes unite,
to bring their sacrifice of praise
before the throne of light;
where God himself creates
a worthy house of prayer,
and his eternal, holy name
will be exalted there.

3. Heaven and earth will pass,
the sea will be no more,
and all the saints, in deathless light,
will worship and adore.
Christ is the first and last,
whose promises are true,
the Alpha and the Omega
who makes creation new.

The Fourth Sunday before Advent

131 CM

1. The great command we would obey,
our God to know and love;
with heart and mind and soul and
strength,
all other things above.

2. The love which we declare for God
is to each other shown;
we share our neighbours' hopes and joys,
their sorrows as our own.

3. And yet, since mortal flesh is weak,
our love cannot suffice,
for loving others as ourselves
demands too high a price.

4. For this our great High Priest has come,
to make the sacrifice,
make whole by grace our broken lives
and pay love's awesome price.

5. His sacrifice, made once for all,
is perfect and complete;
in him creation's finest hopes
for health and wholeness meet.

The Third Sunday before Advent

132 LM

1. Most Holy God we hear your call
from all our Godless ways to turn.
Open our ears to hear your word,
open our hearts that we may learn.

2. Help us to leave the past behind
where it would keep us from your side,
then let the gospel be proclaimed,
God be revealed and glorified.

3. Christ, who has made the sacrifice
no mortal action can repeat;
now, in the fullness of your grace,
perfect redemption is complete.

4. Glory to God, in Christ made known,
suff'ring to set creation free;
now, in the Spirit's pow'r we sing,
'Praise to the holy Trinity.'

The Second Sunday before Advent

133 10 10 11 11

1. In fear and in hope the great day will dawn,
when out of the grave new life will be born;
when judgement and mercy creation refine,
and wisdom and beauty eternally shine.

2. The earth and the heav'ns shall all pass
away,
though none can foretell the hour or the
day.
Through fear and through darkness the
word will endure,
in pow'r and great glory eternally sure.

3. Christ's work is unique, his sacrifice one;
the life he has giv'n for sin will atone.
Eternal perfection his dying achieves,
and Christ from the Father his glory
receives.

Christ the King:
The Sunday Next before Advent

134 **10 11 11 11 and refrain**

1. Christ, come in glory,
with your reign of peace;
let all pain be ended,
all injustice cease.
Come in clouds of heaven,
as the prophet saw,
and, in truth abounding,
let the world adore!

Christ, come in glory,
with your reign of peace;
let all pain be ended,
all injustice cease.

2. Lifted in glory,
reigning from the cross,
give us life abundant
from your bitter loss;
for no earthly kingship
can with yours compare;
painful truth you witness,
thorns and nails you bear!

3. O perfect witness,
first-born from the dead,
purify creation
by the blood you shed.
Alpha and Omega,
all our lives embrace,
in the truth and justice
of your reign of grace.

Year C

First Sunday of Advent

135 87 87 47

1. Holy God, our great redeemer,
give us grace to watch and pray,
'til the sun and stars bear witness
to the long-awaited day;
when triumphant, when triumphant,
truth and freedom come to stay! *(2)*

2. See, the day is surely coming,
promised by divine decree;
joyous day of truth and virtue,
justice and integrity.
God has spoken! God has spoken!
All creation whole and free! *(2)*

3. Come, O God, in liberation;
from our greed we would be free,
filled with love for one another,
and for all humanity;
all creation, all creation,
one in holy liberty. *(2)*

Second Sunday of Advent

136 87 87

1. Let all creation now rejoice,
a song of freedom singing,
proclaiming peace and liberty
from truth and justice springing.

2. We still can hear the prophet's voice
in barren places crying,
'Repent and seek the way of truth,
on God alone relying.'

3. The exiles shall rejoicing come,
from east and west returning,
and God will be their guiding light,
with hope and justice burning.

4. Our God began, and will complete,
the drama of salvation,
as knowledge, hope and love increase,
uniting all creation.

Third Sunday of Advent

137 11 11 11 11

1. As people of God, let us sing and rejoice,
for God our redeemer is giving us voice.
The terror of evil is falling away,
and God joins the dance on the festival day.

2. God gives us our goods and resources to share,
and bids us in commerce and dealings be fair.
In calling the people these ways to embrace,
the prophet announces both judgement and grace.

3. Then let us in patient forbearance abound,
for there may the truest contentment be found;
from fear and resentment our minds will be freed,
and peace yet unknown will fulfil every need.

Fourth Sunday of Advent

138 87 87 D

1. From the humblest of the cities,
Bethlehem, the very least,
comes the Saviour of the nations,
born to rule in truth and peace.
There, among the poor and humble,
justice will be brought to birth;
see the pow'r of love eternal
manifest throughout the earth.

2. Needing not the gifts and praises
our poor worship may afford,
God prepares the perfect offering
of the co-eternal Word:
Word of wholeness and perfection,
now in flesh and blood revealed;
Christ the one, the true oblation,
every sacrifice has sealed.

continued

3. See the hope of liberation,
   by the humble poor received,
   by the Virgin and the barren,
   with such holy joy conceived!
   Mary, mother of salvation,
   full of unexpected grace,
   quicken all our hopes and longings
   by the joy of your embrace.

Christmas Day: Set 1

139 87 87 87

1. Those who walked in deepest darkness
   see at last a splendid light,
   heralding a Son now given,
   born of God to human sight.
   He will reign in peace for ever,
   setting every wrong to right.

2. Shepherds hear the angels calling,
   telling of a newborn King
   lying in a straw-filled manger;
   O, the awesome song they sing!
   'Glory in the highest heaven!'
   All the world with joy will ring!

3. Now, the work of grace completed,
   all creation reconciled,
   let us live in Godly freedom,
   not as slaves by sin defiled;
   seek again the greater glory
   once revealed in Mary's child.

Christmas Day: Set 2

140 10 10 10 10

1. Proclaim good news: God's people have
   been saved,
   this day salvation dawns upon the earth.
   Build up, build up the highway for the
   Lord,
   proclaim God's majesty, and human worth!

2. Proclaim good news: new life is flowing free,
   not by our goodness but by God's own
   grace,
   through Jesus Christ, our Saviour and our
   Lord:
   he pours his Spirit into every place.

3. Proclaim good news: great joy to all the
   world,
   to us is born a Saviour, Christ the Lord.
   'Glory to God!' the angel host proclaim.
   'And peace on earth!' we cry with one
   accord.

Christmas Day: Set 3

141 87 87 87

1. Lovely feet upon the mountains
   bring the distant runner near,
   with the word of true salvation,
   set to gladden every ear.
   Sing for joy, you ransomed people,
   God has made the vision clear.

2. Now in even greater glory
   comes the co-eternal Word,
   he through whom, in primal darkness,
   first creation's breath was stirred.
   All the glory of the Godhead
   in his form is seen and heard.

3. He, the Father's very image,
   came to save and justify,
   then, the full atonement finished,
   took his proper place on high.
   Now his name, with awe and wonder,
   all the angels glorify.

The First Sunday of Christmas

142 LM

1. O God, whose love for all we see
   in that most holy family,
   show us the myst'ry of your grace,
   as freedom flowers in love's embrace!

2. Your gift of love, we now confess,
   is ours to share but not possess.
   Then help us all, in faith and prayer,
   to trust each other to your care.

3. Help us to hear and own the truth,
   when spoken by the lips of youth,
   to welcome their disturbing voice,
   and in your mystery rejoice!

4. O God, whose love for all we see
   most clearly in the Trinity,
   let your mysterious power be known
   to set us free, yet make us one.

The Second Sunday of Christmas

143 84 84 88 84

1. Word made flesh, eternal Wisdom
   born from above,
   light and life of all creation,
   perfect in love;
   faithful to the Father's sending,
   perfectly our nature blending
   by the Spirit's power, attending
   as holy Dove.

2. Come to call your faithful people
   from ev'ry place,
   come to make our hearts your temple,
   radiant with grace;
   come, the Father's love revealing,
   to our wayward souls appealing,
   'til, within his presence kneeling,
   we see his face.

3. Blessèd be our God and Father,
   Saviour and Lord,
   calling us to be his children
   still by his Word,
   who before the world's foundation
   planned our undeserved salvation;
   hail him God of all creation,
   ever adored!

The Epiphany

144 86 88 6

1. Arise to greet the Lord of light,
   you people of his choice.
   In uncreated glory bright,
   he bursts upon our inward sight,
   and bids the heart rejoice! *(2)*

2. Towards his light shall kings be drawn
   this majesty to see,
   and in the brightness of the dawn,
   shall see the longing world reborn
   in justice full and free. *(2)*

3. The holy light in Judah's skies
   calls sages from afar.
   Great minds in meek obedience rise,
   and call the world to recognise
   creation's guiding star! *(2)*

4. This majesty for long concealed
   from longing human sight,
   in Jesus Christ is now revealed,
   and God's eternal promise sealed
   in love's unending light. *(2)*

The Baptism of Christ

145 87 87 87

1. Holy Saviour, God of Israel,
   by whose love we all are made,
   precious in your sight, and honoured,
   we approach you unafraid.
   You, in love, have called and saved us,
   and our ransom you have paid.

2. We have seen your love in action,
   hope reborn and life restored
   by the power of the Spirit,
   and the cleansing water poured.
   Christ, the Word of life abundant,
   be by all the world adored!

continued

3. Not baptised in water only,
   but in Spirit and in fire,
   looking for the consummation
   of the great divine desire,
   let us live in expectation,
   and to higher truth aspire.

The Second Sunday of Epiphany

146 76 76 and refrain

You we praise, O God most high,
your glory we proclaim;
hear the joyful song we sing
in worship to your name.

1. To your unfaithful people,
   you came with grace divine,
   turned life into a wedding,
   and water into wine!

2. The people once rejected,
   unworthy in your sight,
   by grace are now accepted
   to share in your delight!

3. Your one uniting Spirit
   so many gifts has given,
   through all the church expressing
   the promises of heaven.

The Third Sunday of Epiphany

147 87 87 87

1. We have heard the prophet speaking,
   through the pages of the law,
   calling us to celebration
   in the service of the poor.
   Amen, Amen! Amen, Amen!
   Justice to the world restore!

2. Now, with holy pow'r anointed,
   we would set the captive free,
   to the poor, good news proclaiming,
   crying hope and liberty.
   Amen, Amen! Amen, Amen!
   Glory ev'ry eye shall see.

3. Holy Spirit, here unite us,
   our diversity embrace,
   many members, yet one body,
   joined in sacramental grace.
   Amen, Amen! Amen, Amen!
   Speaking peace to ev'ry race.

The Fourth Sunday of Epiphany

148 10 11 11 11 and refrain

1. Love's great endeavour
   praise and glorify:
   faith endures for ever,
   hope will never die.
   God's eternal glory
   shines on every face,
   filling all the temple
   with the light of grace.

   Love's great endeavour
   praise and glorify:
   faith endures for ever,
   hope will never die.

2. Love, all-enduring,
   keeps no count of slights;
   all resentment curing,
   love in truth delights.
   Words of judgement voicing,
   prophets rise and fall,
   love remains, rejoicing,
   faithful to her call.

3. Christ, come in glory
   where your people wait,
   bringing grace and judgement
   both to poor and great.
   Then dismiss your servants,
   in your perfect peace;
   from our age-old burdens
   every soul release.

The Presentation of Christ in the Temple

149 87 87 D

1. Oh, the wonder of the ages,
   God is held in mortal hands,
   offered in an earthly temple
   to fulfil the law's demands!
   With what grace, immortal Being
   shares our flesh and draws our breath,
   by his life true life imparting,
   by his death, destroying death.

2. Lord, transform our earthly temples
   with your covenant of grace,
   make us ready for your coming,
   fit to stand before your face.
   By your own refining presence,
   come to purify and bless,
   that our lives may be an off'ring
   full of truth and righteousness.

3. Come, then, Lord, in grace and
   judgement,
   shaming all our greed and pride,
   to the broken and exploited,
   all the world has cast aside.
   Come, your very self to offer
   to the greatest and the least,
   then present us to the Father,
   Christ, our brother, Saviour, Priest.

Sunday between 3 and 9 February inclusive
(if earlier than the Second Sunday before Lent)

Proper 1

150 CM

1. O God of grace, in glorious state,
   whom seraphim attend,
   here your unworthy servants wait
   for you to call and send.

2. The burning heat of love divine
   can cleanse the faithless heart;
   by simple gifts of bread and wine,
   your healing you impart.

3. Within the world of time and space,
   eternal love is known;
   the sheer abundance of your grace
   in Jesus Christ is shown.

4. Our firm belief we now declare
   in one who died and lives,
   who calls the world your love to share,
   and life eternal gives.

Sunday between 10 and 16 February inclusive
(if earlier than the Second Sunday before Lent)

Proper 2

151 CM

1. Happy are those who trust in you,
   all other things above.
   Help us, O God, to praise your name;
   and lead us in your love.

2. Just as the tree beside the stream
   fears not the summer's heat,
   so, if we rest upon your love,
   our faith can be complete.

3. Since, from the darkness of the grave
   Christ has himself been raised,
   we who have died with him arise
   and sing your glorious praise.

continued

4. Call us, with you, to raise the poor,
   to care for human need,
   'til in a world from greed released,
   Christ Jesus reigns indeed.

Sunday between 17 and 23 February inclusive (if earlier than the Second Sunday before Lent)

Proper 3

152 11 11 10 11

1. 'As you give to others, so you will receive.'
   This is scripture's promise; help us to believe.
   God of compassion, teach us how to live;
   out of your abundance, let us freely give.

2. Adam, in creation, mortal life was given,
   but the second Adam knew the life of heaven.
   God of compassion, Adam's children take,
   fill us with your Spirit, and our lives remake.

3. Let us not, in anger, spiteful vengeance seek,
   rather, words of kindness and forgiveness speak.
   God of compassion, fill us with your grace,
   seeking only goodness in each other's face.

4. Greater joy in giving help us all to learn,
   sharing our resources, asking no return.
   God of compassion, and of liberty,
   from possessions' burdens set our spirits free.

The Second Sunday before Lent

153 DSM

1. God of creative pow'r
   who formed and shaped the earth,
   whose spirit filled the human frame
   with dignity and worth,
   unite us in your love,
   and make us, by your grace,
   one flesh, one bone, one common life,
   one holy human race.

2. God of redemptive pow'r
   we turn to you in prayer,
   when chaos-waters overwhelm
   this fragile boat we share.
   Then let us hear your voice,
   that calls its rage to cease,
   and fills our faithless, mortal hearts
   with wonder, hope and peace.

3. God of eternal pow'r
   in awesome majesty,
   your high eternal praise resounds
   across the crystal sea.
   'All glory to our God,
   who made the heavens and earth!'
   Let all created lips acclaim
   your honour, might and worth.

The Sunday next before Lent

154 DCM

1. The glory of the living Lord
   on Sinai's mount, was shown,
   though not contained in written word
   on bare, unyielding stone;
   for shining in the prophet's face,
   the light of hope foretold
   that greater Word, that nobler grace
   than law can ever hold!

2. Another time and mountain top;
   the glory stands revealed:
   the long-awaited Word of grace
   in flesh and blood concealed!
   Here Moses and Elijah stand,
   the prophet and the law,
   with him, whose outstretched, bleeding hand
   their glory will restore!

3. The written word on lifeless stone,
the face behind the veil,
await a glory yet unknown,
which cannot fade or fail.
The Word incarnate brings to sight
the majesty divine,
whose face, with uncreated light,
eternally will shine!

Ash Wednesday

155 87 87 D

1. Holy God, of righteous glory,
see your people gathered here,
in a solemn congregation,
your forgiving word to hear.
God of love and slow to anger,
gracious, longing to restore,
hear your priests and people calling,
give us grace to sin no more.

2. We confess the pride we suffer,
needs which none can satisfy;
how we love the praise of mortals,
swift to flow'r and quick to die.
Let us find rewards eternal
as we quietly seek your face,
and our open, public living
witness only to your grace.

3. Free us from our self-bound living,
better witnesses to be,
to the world by grace appealing
telling forth the mystery:
how creation's pure Redeemer
walked among us undefiled,
by his deathless love proclaiming,
God with us is reconciled.

The First Sunday of Lent

156 11 12 12 10

1. God, we call upon you; hear us and answer;
rescue us from evil, for grace and pow'r are yours.
From our long enslavement, lead us out to freedom,
and, in compassion, all our lives restore.

2. On the desert journey, tested and tempted,
give us grace and courage, your sacrifice to share,
not for easy glory, comfort or advantage,
seeking to profit from the faith we bear.

3. Keep us ever faithful, always confessing,
both by word and action, the truth our hearts believe.
Then, in love, embracing all without distinction,
life in abundance call us to receive.

The Second Sunday of Lent

157 DSM

1. God of eternal light,
your promises we claim;
as Abram's heirs, we recognise
the honour of your name.
Our sacrifice accept,
our lives of faith inspire,
and every fearful heart transform
with purifying fire.

2. 'Blessed is he who comes
in God's eternal name!'
And yet, this glad, exultant cry
is touched by fear and shame.
Too often have we scorned
the challenge of the word,
and those you sent to voice your call
our anger have incurred.

continued

3. Christ, from the heavens descend,
make life eternal known,
and all our mortal bodies change
to copies of your own.
Creation then shall see
your great and glorious light,
when truth and peace are all around,
and justice burning bright.

Third Sunday of Lent

158 76 76 D

1. The voice of grace and judgement
cries out across the land:
'The feast of life is ready,
prepared by God's own hand.
Why pay for passing pleasures
that cannot satisfy?
God offers food eternal,
and freely will supply.'

2. We follow in the footsteps
of Moses' ancient race,
who, in the Red Sea waters,
received baptismal grace.
The rock provided water
to nourish mind and soul,
yet many, still rebellious,
would fail to reach their goal.

3. We stand as equal sinners,
dependent on your grace;
we come in true repentance
to seek your saving face.
O God of hope, release us
to walk the kingdom's ways,
'til all the world rejoices
to offer perfect praise.

The Fourth Sunday of Lent

159 98 98

1. We celebrate the new creation,
to God, in Christ, now reconciled,
and recognise our full salvation
in him whom people once reviled.

2. In token of our liberation,
within God's presence now we stand,
to share the banquet of salvation,
the harvest of the promised land.

3. The news of reconciliation
is now entrusted to our care.
So spread the word throughout creation,
the feast is here for all to share.

4. Begin the joyful celebration:
the lost return, the dead arise,
to see the light of exultation
which shines from God's forgiving eyes.

Mothering Sunday

160 SM

1. O God of perfect love,
your promises we own,
that through a mother's tender care
your glory can be shown.

2. Then give us faith to know
your word will never fail:
the troubles of the present day
a brighter future veil.

3. The temple prophet speaks,
and we his vision see,
of pain and blessings both to come
in every family.

4. May Mary's faith be found
in ev'ry human heart,
to wonder at the mystery
and play our humble part.

The Fifth Sunday of Lent

161 LM

1. Great God, who opened up the sea,
   and led your ransomed people through,
   help us to leave the past behind,
   and find our life and hope in you.

2. Let all-forgiving love redeem
   our mean and petty-minded ways,
   and penitential tears combine
   with costly love and fragrant praise.

3. Yet, all the worship of the worlds,
   the riches of all time and space,
   cannot begin to represent
   your sheer extravagance of grace.

4. So help us leave, with willing hearts,
   the worldly wealth we count as dross,
   for life in all its glory shines
   beyond the shadow of the cross.

Palm Sunday: Liturgy of the Passion

162 SM

1. What dreadful sight is this,
   by fear and envy wrought,
   the faithful servant of the Lord
   in pain and death distraught!

2. But God will give him strength,
   with patience to endure,
   and bring him through this time of trial
   in word and action pure.

3. And now, before our eyes,
   a myst'ry so divine;
   redemption's wondrous story, told
   in broken bread and wine!

4. The co-eternal Son,
   in splendour bright arrayed,
   for us his glory set aside
   and unto death obeyed.

5. Exalted over all,
   and giv'n the highest name,
   him shall all nations, kings and powers
   eternally acclaim.

Maundy Thursday

163 14 14 4 7 8

1. God of the Passover, Author and Lord
   of salvation,
   gladly we gather to bring you our hearts'
   adoration;
   ransomed and free,
   called and commissioned to be
   signs of your love for creation.

2. Here we remember that evening of
   wonder enthralling,
   myst'ry of passion divine, and betrayal
   appalling.
   Breaking the bread,
   'This is my body,' he said.
   'Do this, my passion recalling.'

3. God of the Eucharist, humbly we gather
   before you,
   and, at your table, for pardon and
   grace we implore you.
   Under the cross,
   counting as profit our loss,
   deep in its shade, we adore you.

Good Friday

164 84 84 88 84

1. Day of wrath and day of wonder,
   whence hope has fled!
   See the body torn asunder,
   blood freely shed.
   Stripped of majesty we saw him,
   human sight recoiled before him,
   yet it was our sorrows tore him;
   for us he bled.

continued

2. Day of hope and day of glory,
 though unperceived!
 See redemption's dreadful story,
 long, long conceived.
 Evil pow'rs in tatters lying,
 knowing death itself is dying,
 hear the voice triumphant crying,
 'All is achieved!'

3. Day of majesty and splendour,
 here ends the race!
 Christ, our Priest, our souls' defender,
 longs to embrace.
 He who walked this earth before us,
 tried and tempted, yet victorious,
 calls us to the kingdom glorious.
 O, perfect grace!

Easter Day

165 CM or 86 86 extended

1. To him who died is now restored
 the life he freely gave.
 We worship here the Lord of life,
 now risen, risen, risen,
 risen from the grave!

2. The misty light of early dawn
 reveals an empty cave.
 How vain to search the tomb for one
 now risen, risen, risen,
 risen from the grave!

3. His were the hands that healed the sick,
 and made the fearful brave.
 Though once despised, his power we see
 now risen, risen, risen,
 risen from the grave!

4. The pleasures of this passing age
 cannot our souls enslave;
 for true contentment rests with him,
 now risen, risen, risen,
 risen from the grave!

5. To all creation, we proclaim,
 'The pow'r to heal and save
 is vested in the living Lord
 now risen, risen, risen,
 risen from the grave!'

The Second Sunday of Easter

166 76 76 D

1. Blest be the God and Father
 of Jesus Christ our Lord,
 for hope to sinners given
 through his unfailing word;
 the promise of redemption
 eternally is sealed,
 and Christ in deathless glory
 by broken tomb revealed.

2. In many signs and wonders,
 his Godly state was shown,
 yet such a Son of David
 the world chose not to own.
 When worldly pow'rs condemned him
 to torture, cross and grave,
 God raised him up and crowned him
 with cosmic pow'r to save.

3. Although we have not seen it,
 his promise we believe;
 what minds can never capture
 our hearts by faith receive.
 Our spirits thirst with longing,
 like infants at the breast,
 to see the Saviour's glory,
 and in his presence rest.

The Third Sunday of Easter

167 76 76 D

1. O God of life and vision, renew our
 failing sight,
 let hearts and minds be open to
 resurrection light;
 come, challenge and restore us, and
 call us to proclaim,
 in free and glad obedience, your life-
 renewing name.

2. You meet us in the presence of failure and regret,
to mortal eyes revealing a greater glory yet;
and those who once have fallen, to wholeness you restore;
the word of pardon lifts us to life for evermore.

3. Then, 'To the Lamb be glory!' the shining hosts proclaim,
and all creation honours the life-renewing name.
Ten thousand times ten thousand, and countless thousands more,
the great 'Amen!' re-echo and joyfully adore.

The Fourth Sunday of Easter

168 87 87 D

1. Sing the gospel of salvation,
tell it out to all the earth;
where the pow'rs of death are reigning,
speak of hope and human worth.
Where our lives by grief are darkened,
locked in death's mysterious night,
hear his call to rise and witness
to abundant life and light.

2. Christ, the one eternal Shepherd,
calls creation to rejoice.
Let the world, in hope and gladness,
recognise salvation's voice.
All who recognise the Saviour
take their place within the fold,
there in perfect truth and freedom,
life's eternal joys to hold.

3. See, the host that none can number
gathers in from every side,
once the victims of injustice,
now redeemed and glorified.
Fear and weeping here are ended,
hunger and oppression cease.
Now the Lamb becomes the shepherd!
Now begins the reign of peace!

The Fifth Sunday of Easter

169 55 54 D

1. 'As 1 have loved you,
love one another;
this is the moment,
this is the place.'
Jesus has spoken
his new commandment,
making us holy,
giving us grace.

2. 'Love one another',
love all creation!
Break down the barriers,
open the door!
Pride is abandoned,
prejudice withers,
petty exclusions
shall be no more.

3. Earth and the heavens
long for renewal,
just as the bridegroom
waits for the bride.
Pain will be ended,
death nonexistent,
God in creation
be glorified.

The Sixth Sunday of Easter

170 77 77 77

1. Holy God, in every place,
let us hear the call of grace.
Open up all human hearts
to the truth your word imparts.
Let our faith's expression be
love and hospitality.

2. Call to mind the way preferred
by the true incarnate Word,
in whose perfect life is shown
grace abundant, love unknown;
lead us into truth divine,
signified in bread and wine.

continued

3. Let us now the vision see
of the city fair and free,
built upon celestial ground,
with eternal glory crowned,
sunless, yet for ever bright,
with the Lamb its only light.

Ascension Day

171 CM

1. The risen Saviour now ascends
toward the highest place,
and offers broken human flesh
before the throne of grace!

2. His blood has opened up the way,
salvation is secure,
and we may stand within the veil
in mind and body pure.

3. Through pain and death to life and hope,
Christ trod the way of love,
and he will clothe the church below
with glory from above.

The Seventh Sunday of Easter

172 DSM

1. Heaven is open wide
where truth and love are found,
and every dark and painful place
is changed to holy ground.
The jailer and the jailed
together are set free,
and, in each other's freedom, find
their perfect liberty.

2. Heaven is open wide,
and perfect love we see,
in God's eternal self revealed:
the blessed Trinity.
Christ for the church has prayed,
that we may all be one,
and share the triune grace, whereby
creation was begun.

3. Heaven is open wide,
and Christ in glory stands:
the Source and End, the First and Last,
with justice in his hands.
Let all the thirsty come,
where life is flowing free,
and Christ, in splendour yet unknown,
our morning star will be.

The Day of Pentecost

173 SM

1. Come, Spirit of our God,
our lives with truth inspire,
and burn within our fearful hearts
like purifying fire.

2. Fill every heart with love;
the word we would obey.
O, teach us all we need to know
of your most holy way.

3. Come with the gift of life,
our nature to refine;
as sons and daughters let us live,
and heirs of love divine.

4. Give us a willing voice
to speak in every place,
wherever doubts and fears confine,
of liberating grace.

Trinity Sunday

174 86 88 6

1. O holy wisdom, found at play
before the world was born,
you danced in light's first dawning ray,
delighting in the primal day
which saw creation's dawn. *(2)*

2. Come, Holy Spirit, gift divine
of Father and of Son;
reveal the truth by word and sign,
and celebrate in bread and wine
the life in God begun. *(2)*

3. Eternal God of time and space,
   create, sustain, restore.
   Through Jesus Christ, by faith and grace,
   let us your patient hope embrace,
   and let the world adore! *(2)*

Sunday between 29 May and 4 June inclusive (if after Trinity Sunday)

Proper 4

175 87 87 87

1. Christ, in every mortal language,
   let your name be glorified;
   give the church the grace to listen
   to the voices from outside.
   Alleluia! Alleluia!
   Shame our narrow-minded pride!

2. To the pagan Roman soldier,
   your authority was known;
   to his voice, your ears were open,
   to his servant, healing shown.
   Alleluia! Alleluia!
   For our prejudice, atone.

3. Let us not confine our vision,
   seeking worthless human praise;
   help us risk ourselves to freedom,
   in your kingdom's open ways.
   Alleluia! Alleluia!
   Every nation tribute pays.

Sunday between 5 and 11 June inclusive (if after Trinity Sunday)

Proper 5

176 87 87 D

1. God of old, who sent the prophet,
   with the life-renewing word,
   full of anger and compassion,
   which the poor and humble heard;
   where the tears of grief are falling,
   hear the church's heartfelt cry,
   with abundant life responding
   to the great resounding 'Why?'

2. God of life, in hope resplendent,
   greet us at the final gate;
   meet the threat of dereliction
   with the power to re-create.
   Feel again the prophet's anger,
   hear again the widow's cries;
   speak at last the word of healing,
   calling us from death to rise.

3. God of hope, you chose and called us,
   from the darkness of the womb
   to the joy of life abundant,
   stronger even than the tomb.
   Harness all our hope and anger
   with the energy of grace,
   joy in life renewed proclaiming,
   forcing open death's embrace.

Sunday between 12 and 18 June inclusive (if after Trinity Sunday)

Proper 6

177 LM

1. Christ, at your table we present
   all that we know of who we are.
   Close to your feet, we worship you,
   not, with foreboding, from afar.

2. All of the things that bring us shame,
   here at your banquet we outpour,
   knowing that penitential hearts
   you, with compassion, will restore.

3. Where, by our use of wealth and power,
   we damage or exploit the weak,
   then, by your all-revealing word,
   call us your clemency to seek.

4. Help us to find your saving grace
   shown through your love and in the law,
   and by the faith that you impart,
   your likeness in our hearts restore.

Sunday between 19 and 25 June inclusive (if after Trinity Sunday)

Proper 7

178 87 87 47

1. O, the myst'ry of salvation
both in grace and judgement shown:
God who calls us to repentance,
God who offers love unknown.
Save your people,
bring us, trembling, to your throne. *(2)*

2. God will call to life and freedom
souls by fear and death confined.
Every mind and heart held captive,
his compassion can unbind.
Break our shackles,
clothe us in our proper mind. *(2)*

3. By our faith in Christ united,
no distinctions now we see,
here uniting all the cultures,
male and female, slave and free.
By his passion, by his passion,
he has won our liberty. *(2)*

Sunday between 26 June and 2 July inclusive

Proper 8

179 76 76 and refrain

Holy God, we hear your call,
and follow where you lead.
From our self-indulgent lives
our spirits you have freed.

1. Elisha, at the furrow,
Elijah's summons heard,
and sacrificed his future,
responding to your word.

2. In Christ, you stand before us,
and call us to decide;
the challenge of the kingdom
all else must override.

3. The Spirit calls and guides us
our selfish ways to leave,
and, loving one another,
the highest joy receive.

Sunday between 3 and 9 July inclusive

Proper 9

180 666 66 and refrain

1. Holy God, give us peace,
let hope flower, love increase;
grace and truth now release,
like a river flowing,
through the nations growing.

Give us peace and joy,
give us peace and joy,
God of truth, God of hope,
God of love eternal.

2. Send us out to proclaim
peace and truth in your name;
still the word is the same:
'God in mercy sends us,
and in hope befriends us.'

3. In the cross is our pride,
to the world crucified,
sing of grace far and wide,
Christ is our salvation;
join the new creation!

Sunday between 10 and 16 July inclusive

Proper 10

181 10 10 11 11

1. Creator of all, your word we acclaim,
and seek, in our lives, to honour your name.
Not distant or hidden, but close as the
heart,
the word all-revealing its truth will impart.

2. Your statute of love in Jesus we see,
and neighbours to all he calls us to be.
In places of danger, the broken we seek,
and risk our resources defending the weak.

3. Give glory to Christ, and honour and worth,
uniting all things in heaven and earth.
We join with the saints who rejoice in his sight,
and share in his kingdom of freedom and light.

Sunday between 17 and 23 July inclusive

Proper 11

182 CM

1. Heal us, O God, our only help;
our lives' foundation prove,
and let us bring, with willing hearts,
a sacrifice of love.

2. Call us to open up our lives,
our worldly goods to share,
and in your name to eat and drink
with angels unaware.

3. Come and be welcome in our homes,
as our most honoured guest,
and in life's bustle give us grace
to listen and to rest.

4. O, what a myst'ry, O, what love
your scars, Lord Christ, reveal!
You send us out in glorious hope,
creation's wounds to heal.

Sunday between 24 and 30 July inclusive

Proper 12

183 888

1. O God, within this special place,
we pray for strength, for hope and grace,
to trust our lives to your embrace.

2. Like Abraham, we dare to plead
for people in their special need,
as for the world we intercede.

3. O, hear our long, persistent cry
for all who in oppression die,
where greed and envy crucify.

4. In grace and freedom, may we pray,
through Christ who died, our debts to pay,
and now to life has led the way.

5. O Christ, perfect your gift of grace,
transcend the bounds of time and space,
uniting every tribe and race.

Sunday between 31 July and 6 August inclusive

Proper 13

184 11 12 12 10

1. Wisdom of the ages, help us and save us
from the stress and straining that fill our waking hours.
Vanity ensnares us, fame and wealth enslave us,
futile injustice drains our vital pow'rs.

2. Greater, ever greater, grows our ambition,
larger, ever larger, our warehouses and stores.
How we love possessions, long for recognition!
Greed, in its blindness, deeper needs ignores.

3. Let us follow Jesus, share in his dying,
crucify the longings which hinder and enthral,
peace and justice loving, wholeness glorifying,
'til, in perfection, Christ is all in all.

Sunday between 7 and 13 August inclusive

Proper 14

185 11 11 10 11

1. God of hope and promise, give us grace to hear,
follow where you lead us, through our doubt and fear.
Ready and waiting may we ever be,
trusting your assurance where we cannot see.

2. Keep your servants watchful, waiting your return;
when the night is darkest, brightest lamps must burn;
ready and waiting, knowing not the hour,
longing for the kingdom's liberating power.

3. Only faith sustains us in the hope we hold,
waiting for the promised blessings to unfold.
Ready and waiting, help us to believe,
old and poor and barren will your gift conceive.

4. Strangers, nomads, pilgrims, on the earth we roam,
while our hearts are longing for a better home;
ready and waiting, confident to see
all injustice righted, and creation free.

Sunday between 14 and 20 August inclusive

Proper 15

186 76 76 D

1. O God, renew our vision, and help us to discern
the truth and honest wisdom with which your prophets burn.
Then let our words and actions uphold your righteous name
confronting all creation with your compelling claim.

2. When kings and politicians abuse their earthly power;
where greed and exploitation make all the world seem sour,
then let us look to Jesus, and run our earthly race,
as earth and heav'n bear witness to his abundant grace.

3. When opposition rises, let us not seek to hide,
or shirk the confrontation that Jesus glorified.
He takes his place in glory by God's eternal throne,
his perfect grace disposing to make creation one.

Sunday between 21 and 27 August inclusive

Proper 16

187 DSM

1. God, be our constant guide,
and meet our deepest need,
to live as people of your light,
from all oppression freed.
O let our praise be true,
our worship not in vain,
delighting in integrity,
not seeking selfish gain.

2. Here in this holy place,
we hold our heads up high,
as those whom Christ has touched and healed,
our lives to dignify.
Let no one be afraid
to stand within this place,
for all are equal in his sight,
as sinners saved by grace.

3. Now let our praise be joined
   with worship in the height,
   where countless angels celebrate
   with all the saints in light:
   the city of our God;
   so tremble, heav'n and earth,
   and let the universe declare
   his high eternal worth.

Sunday between 28 August and 3 September inclusive

Proper 17

188 77 77 77

1. God of true humility,
   humble servants we would be.
   Save us then from vain conceit;
   make the work of grace complete.
   Open each attentive ear
   your eternal truth to hear.

2. Let us share your royal feast
   with the poorest and the least,
   who cannot our gifts return;
   let them be our chief concern,
   giving them a higher place
   in the order of your grace.

3. Here let love divine be found,
   let this place be holy ground,
   as for others' needs we care,
   serving angels, unaware.
   Thus let all our lives proclaim
   Christ, for evermore the same.

Sunday between 4 and 10 September inclusive

Proper 18

189 87 87 87

1. God of life, you bless your people
   by the challenge of your voice:
   'Life or death, and curse or blessing,'
   we are called to make our choice.
   With the blessèd life of heaven,
   let creation all rejoice.

2. Shame the world's possessive madness
   by the wisdom of the cross;
   from the prisons which 'secure' us,
   set us free to suffer loss.
   Give us grace to be disciples,
   and the strength to bear the cost.

3. Let us learn to live together
   as your people, not as slaves,
   holding, helping and releasing
   everyone who freedom craves;
   looking to the risen Saviour,
   whose compassion heals and saves.

Sunday between 11 and 17 September inclusive

Proper 19

190 10 11 11 12

1. God of forgiveness, your people you freed,
   and saw them return to idolatrous greed;
   with anger against them, you righteously
   burned,
   but then to compassion and forgiveness
   you turned.

2. God of forgiveness, the Saviour you sent,
   proclaiming good news, with the call to
   repent.
   With merciful love and forgiveness he
   came,
   the lost and the headstrong to embrace
   and reclaim.

3. God of forgiveness, your pow'r we implore,
   with mercy and wholeness, our lives to
   restore.
   Perverse and misguided, our souls we
   deprave;
   O come, full of healing, with compassion
   to save.

Sunday between 18 and 24 September inclusive

Proper 20

191 DCM

1. The word of God rings harsh and clear:
the judgement will be great
on those who trade dishonestly,
and tamper with the weight.
'You wish the Sabbath day were gone,
its spirit you ignore;
you long to prey upon the weak
and buy and sell the poor.'

2. The Saviour said, 'You cannot serve
both God and money, too;
you will be faithless to the one,
and to the other true.'
Then let us all for God alone,
in freedom make our choice,
and in the things of greatest worth
eternally rejoice.

3. Now to the God of perfect love
let praise and prayers ascend,
for justice in the present world
and mercy at the end.
For people in authority
your wisdom we implore,
who stewards of your love must be,
defenders of the poor.

Sunday between 25 September and 1 October inclusive

Proper 21

192 CM

1. The rich in splendid castle homes,
the poor ones at the gate,
God has created equally,
and hates their unjust state.

2. The word of warning comes to all
who others' needs ignore,
who live in luxury untold,
provided by the poor!

3. The prophets all proclaimed the word
of judgement, grace and fear,
but those for whom the word is meant
are not inclined to hear.

4. The saintly life which God commands
would untold wealth release,
and hasten in the glorious time
of justice and of peace.

Sunday between 2 and 8 October inclusive

Proper 22

193 CM

1. 'How long, O God,' the people cry,
'must poverty prevail,
while wars and famines come and go
and all our efforts fail?'

2. The world we see appears devoid
of reason and of rhyme,
but faith will keep the vision bright,
'til comes the promised time.

3. We see our faith as small and weak,
and long for it to grow,
yet even such a tiny seed
may great achievements know.

4. So kindle here the gift of faith,
and fan it to a flame,
then justice, truth and liberty
will glorify God's name.

Sunday between 9 and 15 October inclusive

Proper 23

194 CM

1. God of creation, with what joy
your goodness we proclaim!
Your love is freely shown to all
who do not know your name.

2. Those whom the world has called unclean
you gladly touch and hold;
and all who, from a distance, cry,
your open arms enfold.

3. Nothing you ask of us but love;
your grace we cannot earn.
You freely give yourself to those
who never thanks return.

4. Let us declare this gospel word,
but not for worldly gain;
we look towards the promised time
of love's unhindered reign.

Sunday between 16 and 22 October inclusive

Proper 24

195 98 98

1. Eternal God, you cry for justice,
and call the church that cry to share;
so some engage in mortal combat,
and some in agonising prayer.

2. The human judge, for peace and quiet,
will heed the widow's constant cry,
but you, O God, for pure compassion,
to our petition will reply.

3. Then give us grace, when all seems futile,
in hopeful prayer to persevere,
our hopes, our dreams, our failures bringing
to you, who all our prayers will hear.

4. So may we call the world to freedom,
confronting all who would oppose,
with faith and hope, the truth proclaiming,
'til justice through creation flows.

Sunday between 23 and 29 October inclusive

Proper 25

196 CM

1. Come, holy God, and cleanse our souls
of every trace of pride,
and in humility of heart
may you be glorified.

2. The humble poor, in every age,
to you present their case;
you listen to the widow's prayer,
the orphan you embrace.

3. The sinner to your presence comes,
with penitential plea,
and finds in your redeeming word
forgiveness flowing free.

4. So by your power, eternal God,
the gospel we proclaim,
and, from the depths of humble hearts,
we praise your saving name.

All Saints' Day

197 DSM

1. Firm in the faith of God
the saints have lived and died,
who with the Son in glory stand,
redeemed and purified.
This is the glorious hope
in which our hearts abound,
to look upon the face of God
with love eternal crowned.

2. Blessèd are those who long
for freedom, love and peace,
who long to see the truth prevail
and all injustice cease.
The humble and the poor,
and those who weep or mourn,
shall rise with all the saints to see
the new creation's dawn.

3. Stir up the winds of heav'n,
the oceans and the tide,
and let your kingdom come, O God,
your love be glorified.
Let all creation hear
the challenge of your voice,
and in the vision of your peace
eternally rejoice.

The Fourth Sunday before Advent

198 55 54 D

1. God of salvation, longing for justice,
   let not our worship ever be vain:
   challenge injustice, show your compassion,
   join in your protest, share your campaign.

2. Christ, our redeemer, sinners restoring,
   giving the guilty hope and respect,
   move us and melt us, love us and lift us,
   giving us grace we dare not expect.

3. God, we adore you, worship and wonder,
   praise and repentance lay at your feet.
   Seek us and save us, rest and redeem us,
   grace us with goodness, make us complete.

The Third Sunday before Advent

199 SM

1. O listen to our prayer,
   great God of all who live,
   and to the pleading of our hearts
   a timely answer give.

2. When evil forces rage,
   then let us faithful stay,
   for from oppression's darkest night
   comes resurrection's day.

3. Let all the world rejoice,
   for Christ has set us free
   from paralysing fear of death,
   for life and liberty.

4. This gospel we believe,
   that Christ has lived and died,
   and all who will accept his call
   with him are glorified.

The Second Sunday before Advent

200 LM

1. The dreaded day will surely dawn,
   in judgement awesome and divine,
   and at its heart, with healing rays,
   the Sun of righteousness will shine.

2. The gracious judgement of our God
   will set oppression's victims free,
   and all who patiently endure
   will live for all eternity.

3. The pow'rs and rulers of this world
   will call on us to make our case;
   on God alone we will rely,
   and trust the all-sufficient grace.

4. So let us fully play our part,
   for wholeness and for liberty,
   'til Christ is known throughout the world,
   and all creation glad and free.

Christ the King:
The Sunday next before Advent

201 10 11 11 11 and refrain

1. Christ reigns triumphant,
   worldly splendour pales!
   See the throne of glory,
   made from wood and nails!
   Let the powerful mock him,
   let the thief deride;
   hist'ry will remember
   Jesus glorified!

   Christ reigns triumphant,
   worldly splendour pales!
   See the throne of glory,
   made from wood and nails!

2. Christ, Son of David,
   Shepherd of the sheep,
   in this glorious shadow
   all your people keep.
   By the pain you suffer,
   bring creation peace,
   and from fear and malice
   every heart release.

3. Likeness and image
   of the God of light,
   robed in scarlet splendour,
   awesome to our sight;
   first-born of creation,
   first-born from the grave,
   from the powers of darkness
   all creation save!

Index of Hymns for the Common Worship Lectionary

Metrical Index